MiG KILL

Lieutenant (j.g.) Philip Vampatella felt his F-8E Crusader shudder as it took a hit from flak. Shortly afterwards, the young Navy pilot saw a MiG-17 closing from the classic six o'clock position, directly astern. Wrapping his plane into a tight diving turn Vampatella headed for the ground, his stricken aircraft bucking and yawing. With his altitude right down to the trees he pulled out of his dive and apparently lost the MiG. But when he settled down and looked around he saw his would-be attacker evidently headed for home.

Quickly deciding against returning to the carrier to replenish his fuel supply which was nearly gone, Vampatella went after the MiG. He closed rapidly on his prey, fired off a Sidewinder and watched the North Vietnamese plane disappear in a large cloud of smoke.

Then he turned for home where he arrived safely and found that his tail had taken a direct hit from a 37-mm antiaircraft burst with about eighty smaller shrapnel holes dotting his Crusader's surfaces.

THE NAVAL AIR WAR IN VIETNAM

BY PETER B. MERSKY & NORMAN POLMAR

ZEBRA BOOKS
KENSINGTON PUBLISHING CORP.

ZEBRA BOOKS

are published by

Kensington Publishing Corp.
475 Park Avenue South
New York, NY 10016

First Zebra Books printing: January 1986

Printed in the United States of America

Cover photo courtesy of U.S. Navy & Peter B. Mersky

This book is for Lieutenant Commander Eliot F. Tozer III, who served his country during Vietnam as a carrier pilot and who later shared with one of the authors his love of flying; Lieutenant Commander Tozer was killed in a training accident off the carrier *Kitty Hawk* in August 1980.

Contents

Foreword

The authors provide the reader with the most complete chronicle of the air war in Vietnam yet to be published. From the outset, this book provides an in-depth examination of the factors leading to this philosophically divisive war and a personally involving account of how it was waged, won, and lost.

The book offers a vivid description of what that war was to the warrior in the sky and how he performed. Also explained are the often discussed, but little understood constraints placed on him by those military leaders in crucial decision making positions far from the scenes of the war. There is also another theme in the book: once combat is joined, the military commander on the scene is the best and in some respects the only person qualified to make tactical decisions.

This book provides a highly accurate perception of what that war was really like, devoid of the emotions of those at home but vociferously opposing U.S. participation in the war. And, it is in this area that Messrs. Polmar and Mersky are at their best, portraying with exacting detail vignettes from the lives of many participants. They highlight the personal involvement of these individuals in this frustrating off-again, on-again conflict. The reliance and the interdependence upon one another which developed among the men in the sky, plus the knowledge that they were continually at the leading edge of their profession created a camaraderie among these men that counterbalanced the confusion, frustration, and hurt caused by the critics of their efforts.

Among the many naval aviators whose experiences are described in this book is then-Lieutenant Elliot Tozer III, an A-4 Skyhawk pilot. An excerpt from his war diary quoted in the book reads, in part, "The frustration comes on all levels. We fly a limited aircraft, drop limited ordnance, on rare targets in a severely limited amount of time. Worst of all, we do all this in a limited and highly unpopular war. . . . All theories aside, what I've got is personal pride pushing against a tangled web of frustration."

That tells most of the story, and this fine book tells most of the remainder of the naval air war in Vietnam.

Vice Admiral Wesley L. McDonald,
US Navy
Deputy Chief of Naval Operations
(Air Warfare)
June 1981

(*Publisher's note*: Admiral McDonald's participation in the Vietnam War began in August 1964 when, as Commanding Officer of Attack Squadron 56, he flew air cover for the destroyer *Maddox* in the Gulf of Tonkin to help fend off PT-boat attacks. He returned to the war as Commander Carrier Airwing 15 aboard the *Coral Sea,* then as Commanding Officer of the *Coral Sea*, and in 1972-74 as Commander Carrier Division Three.)

Preface

The Vietnam War — American combat in the Indochina peninsula — began in 1964 with the attack by North Vietnamese torpedo boats against U.S. surface ships in the Gulf of Tonkin, and ended eleven years later with the hurried evacuation of Americans from South Vietnam in 1975. The war was in large part a naval war and in large part an air war. U.S. naval aviation was involved from start to finish, from flying protective air cover for the destroyers in the Gulf of Tonkin and carrying out the reactive raids against PT-boat bases in the North, until the last-minute removal of Americans and key South Vietnamese personnel from Saigon.

This book seeks to provide an overview of the participation of U.S. naval aviation in the war. The U.S. Navy has its own, integral air arm, larger than most of the world's air forces. Essentially all segments of naval aviation were employed in Vietnam — carrier-based aircraft, land-based and flying boat patrol planes, cargo and transport aircraft, Marine aviation, and, of course, hundreds of the ubiquitous Navy and Marine helicopters. But the war was also fought by the less publicized reconnaissance, electronic surveillance, and search-and-rescue aircraft, and we have sought to illuminate their activities and to put them in perspective.

The Vietnam War was a long and costly one for the United States, costly in lives, resources, and psychological trauma. Naval aviation shared in those costs while, at the same time, carrying out its military missions, most with considerable success.

The authors are in debt to many individuals for their assistance in writing and editing this book.

Major Frank Batha, USMC, and Robert Cressman of the Marine Historical Center; Commander Robert Beck, VA-113; Major Knox Bishop, USAF, 72nd StratWing, Andersen AFB, Guam; Commander T.C. Irwin, Commander Cary Carson and Lieutenant Commander Jake Jacobi, VF-24; Gunnery Sergeant William Judge, USMC; Robert Chenoweth of the Naval Aviation History Office; Commander Richard Coffman, Commander Jay Miller, Commander Louis R. Mortimer, Commander Doug Simpson, Commander James Ozbirn and Lieutenant Commander Tom Nelson, VFP-63; Commander Larry Poe, Chief Photographers Mate Gary Hill and Tom Foley, VAP-61; Captain Richard Knott, VP-16; Ed Marolda of the Naval Historical Center; Captain Richard K. Maughlin, VF-211; Commander Daniel E. Moylan, VA-105; Stephen D. Oltmann, who prepared the maps; Captain S. "Pete" Purvis, VF-151; Captain R. Rausa, VA-25; Lieutenant Commander Merrill Waits, VAQ-132; and Mrs. Eliot F. Tozer III.

Others who gave their assistance are: Commander Robert Norrell, Commander John Kuchinski, as well as Robert A. Carlisle and his assistant, Yeoman Second Class Evelyn Jutte of the Office of Information, Navy Department; Ed Michalski and his assistant, Miss Betty Sprigg, of the Office of the Assistant Secretary of Defense (Public Affairs); Sandy Russell of *Naval Aviation News*: and Mrs. Louise Rigney.

The authors also wish to thank Gordon Swanborough and J.W.R. Taylor, whose publications provided historical and numerical data, and Robert Lawson, editor of *The Hook*.

Glossary

AAA	Antiaircraft Artillery
ACV	Air Cushion Vehicle
Alpha Strike	A large offensive air strike, involving all the carrier wing's assets, fighters, attack, refueling, etc.
BARCAP	Barrier Combat Air Patrol. A fighter patrol between the carrier task force and enemy threat
CAG	Air group commander. A somewhat archaic term, as wing designation was changed to CVW, and commander was subsequently referred to as a CAW; but CAG title remained part of the vocabularly.
CAP	Combat Air Patrol
COD	Carrier On-board Delivery. Usually C-1 and C-2 aircraft which delivered mail, supplies and personnel to carriers while ships were underway.
CV	Aircraft Carrier
CVA	Attack Aircraft Carrier
CVAN	Attack Aircraft Carrier (nuclear-pro-

	pelled)
CVS	Antisubmarine Aircraft Carrier
CVW	Carrier Air Wing
ECM	Electronic Countermeasures
GCI	Ground-Controlled Intercept
HM	Navy Helicopter Mine Countermeasures Squadron (CH-53 Sea Stallion)
HMH	Heavy Marine Helicopter Squadron (CH-53 Sea Stallion)
HMM	Medium Marine Helicopter Squadron (CH-34 Seabat and CH-46 Sea Knight)
IOIC	Integrated Operational Intelligence Center
IR	Infrared. Applicable to heat-seeking Sidewinder missile or to special film used to detect heat sources on ground.
LSO	Landing Signal Officer
LZ	Landing Zone
MAG	Marine Aircraft Group
MiG	Acronym formed by last names of two major Soviet aircraft designers, Mikoyan and Gurevich
MiG CAP	Standing patrol over the fleet or strike force to protect against any threat by enemy aircraft
PIRAZ	Positive Identification Radar Advisory Zone. A ship stationed on a rotational basis in the Tonkin Gulf, providing navigational, weather, and threat information for Navy and Air Force aircraft.
Reece	Shortened form for Reconnaissance
Red Crown	Similar to PIRAZ but tasked specifi-

	cally with providing threat information
RESCAP	Rescue Combat Air Patrol
RVAH	Navy Heavy Reconnaissance Squadron (RA-5C Vigilante)
RVAW	Navy Carrier Airborne Early Warning Squadron (E-1 Tracer and E-2 Hawkeye)
SAM	Surface-to-Air Missile. A generic term, but usually referring to Soviet-built
S A 2	SA-2 Guideline
SAR	Search and Rescue
SARCAP	Search and Rescue Combat Air Patrol
SATS	Short Airfield for Tactical Support
TARCAP	Target Combat Air Patrol. Fighters tasked with providing escort protection for the strike force
Trap	An arrested landing aboard a carrier
VA	Navy Attack Squadron (A-4 Skyhawk, A-1 Skyraider, A-6 Intruder, A-7 Corsair)
VAH	Navy Heavy Attack Squadron (A-3B Skywarrior)
VAP	Navy Heavy Photographic Squadron (RA-3B Skywarrior)
VAQ	Navy Tactical Electronic Warfare Squadron (EKA-3 Skywarrior later EA-6B Prowler)
VF	Navy Fighter Squadron (F-4 Phantom or F-8 Crusader)
VFP	Navy Light Photographic Squadron (RF-8 Crusader)
VMA	Marine Attack Squadron (A-4 Skyhawk)

VMA(AW)	Marine All-Weather Attack Squadron (A-6 Intruder)
VMCJ	Marine Composite Reconnaissance Squadron (EF-10B Skyknight, RF-4B Phantom, EA-6A Intruder, and EA-6B Prowler, providing photographic and ECM services)
VMFA	Marine Fighter and Attack Squadron (F-4 Phantom)
VMF(AW)	Marine All-Weather Fighter Squadron (F-8 Crusader, later F-4 Phantom)
VMO	Marine Observation Squadron (UH-1 helicopter, later OV-10 Broncos)
VO	Navy Observation Squadron (OP-2E Neptune)
VP	Navy Patrol Squadron (P-5 Marlin, P-2 Neptune, P-3 Orion)
VS	Navy Antisubmarine Squadron (S-2 Tracker)

1

Prelude

The planes from *Hancock* and *Ticonderoga* struck hard and fast, shattering tankers, coastal supply barges, and any other enemy vessels they found in Saigon Harbor. The fighters, the best America had to offer its pilots, destroyed fourteen enemy fighters in the air. Aboard his flagship, the carrier *Hancock*, Vice Admiral John S. McCain watched as the burning wreckage of one of the enemy planes tumbled into the sea a few hundred yards away.

The task force had made its way into the South China Sea only three days before, and now, after striking at the heart of the enemy's defenses in Southeast Asia, and then turning north to avoid an approaching typhoon, the carriers refueled from the oilers accompanying the main force, and headed for Formosa and the Philippines. January 12, 1945, had been a very busy day for Task Force 38.

THE FRENCH CONNECTION

Thus, when the bombs and rockets of the aircraft of the *Ticonderoga* and *Constellation* slammed into the North Vietnamese PT-boat bases of Hon Gai and Loc Chao on the afternoon of August 6, 1964, U.S. carrier aviation was no stranger to that troubled area of the world known as Southeast Asia. Indeed, carrier aviation remained an important factor in the region even with the cessation of hostilities following World War II.

As the end of the war approached, the French, aided by the Allies, were beginning to infiltrate Japanese-held Indochina in early 1945. The Japanese could fend off any large-scale takeover, but had trouble containing the efforts of rebel groups seeking their overthrow, especially the Communists, who were known as the Vietminh. The war's end in August 1945 saw the Japanese in control of all Indochina except the area around Hanoi. This the Communists proclaimed as the Democratic Republic of Vietnam. The Japanese were retained under arms by the victorious Allies to police the southern area, but the absence of French troops allowed the Vietminh to gain considerable strength. Thus began the civil war which would engulf the region for nearly thirty years.

By March 1946, the old French carrier *Béarn* to be employed as a troop transport, had been moved up the river to Saigon. As the *Béarn* proceeded north to Haiphong, the old ship came under fire from the Chinese in control of the city, but the French were able to land enough troops to force the

The escort carrier *Dixmunde* was the first flattop to fly aircraft in combat over Vietnam after World War II. American-built, she flew ex-U.S. Navy SBD Dauntless dive bombers in the late 1940s. Here she is shown leaving a U.S. port with a deckload of naval aircraft for transport to Indochina. (U.S. Navy)

Chinese to withdraw by summer. After the Chinese had left, the Vietminh continued their disruptive efforts against the French. By March of 1947, it was necessary to send the escort aircraft carrier *Dixmunde* to Vietnam. Her aircraft, mainly Douglas SBD Dauntless divebombers, late of the U.S. Navy, operated along the Annam region of the Vietnamese coast. The *Dixmunde* stayed off Vietnam until her return to France for repairs in May 1947. She returned in October in time to support a French paratroop assault north of Hanoi, her single squadron of Dauntlesses flying more than 200 sorties and dropping 65 tons of bombs.

A larger French carrier, the *Arromanches*, formerly the British light carrier *Colossus*, took the *Dixmunde*'s place in November 1948, adding the *Dixmunde*'s veteran SBDs to her squadron of Supermarine Seafire IIIs. In a daring move, the *Arromanches* sailed up the Saigon River. She was the largest ship to ever navigate that treacherous body of water, and she faced the added danger of enemy fire from both sides of the banks. However, she arrived at Saigon without incident and for the next ten days her SBDs and Seafires operated from land bases in conjunction with air-force aircraft.

The aging Seafires and SBDs soon reached the limit of their usefulness, and it was not until September 1951 that an operational French carrier strike force was returned to the South China Sea. The *Dixmunde* had gone to the United States and returned carrying a deckload of more modern Grumman F6F Hellcats and Curtiss SB2C Helldivers. Coming out of overhaul at about the

The French carrier *Arromanches*, a former British light carrier, is seen here steaming up the Saigon River to the capital of South Vietnam. Naval aviation—both carrier-based and land-based—played a major role in supporting French ground operations in Indochina. Most of the aircraft available to the French in the late 1940s were obsolescent. Only after the United States became involved in the Korean War in 1950 were more modern aircraft made available to the French. (French Navy)

same time as the *Dixmunde*'s arrival, the *Arromanches* appropriated her sister carrier's aircraft, operating for seven months off the coast and flying more than 670 sorties in support of French forces in Indochina.

Arromanches shuttled back and forth to France, using her Hellcats and Helldivers to disrupt the Communist supply lines. French carrier strength was augmented by the arrival in June 1951 of the

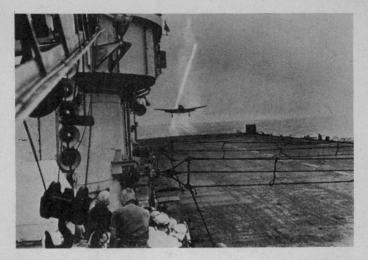

An SB2C Helldiver comes in for a landing aboard the French carrier *Arromanches*. In the foreground are wire barriers, to halt the aircraft should it miss the arresting wires. Before the development of angled or canted flight decks, a plane that missed the arresting wires would crash into planes forward if not halted by the barrier. (French Navy)

La Fayette, formerly the United States carrier *Langley* (CVL-27). The *La-Fayette* operated her F6F Hellcats and SB2C Helldivers alongside the *Arromanches* squadrons.

French carrier aviation continued to support the ground troops against the Vietminh until 1954, when the debacle of Dienbienphu sealed the fate of French colonialism in Indochina. French aviators found it difficult to aid their comrades in this battle. The fortress of Dienbienphu was 170 miles west of Hanoi, the nearest major French air base; this was at the extreme limit of air-support range.

Nor did the rainy spring weather help matters. French supply to the beleaguered troops holding out for over five months slowed to a trickle.

Nevertheless, the French pilots tried. The land-based B-26s, PB4Y Privateers, and (another U.S. Navy discard) F8F Bearcats flew with *Aeronavale* Grummans and Curtisses through veritable curtains of flak and small arms to relieve the men on the ground. It was a scene strangely foreboding of similar situations faced by U.S. fliers ten years later. The relief effort force was augmented by the Chance Vought AU-1, one of the final versions of the gull-winged F4U Corsair, delivered to the French forces in Da Nang in April 1954.

The light carrier *La Fayette*, a former U.S. CVL, and the *Arromanches* provided air support to French forces during the final, tragic efforts to restore French control to Indochina in the early 1950s. Shown in Indochina in March 1955 in this view, her deck is loaded with F4U Corsairs. (French Navy)

The Eisenhower Administration denied a French plea for air strikes on Dienbienphu from U.S. fleet carriers off the coast. The U.S. Navy carriers steamed up and down the South China Sea, their decks loaded with modern jet aircraft; but they were not allowed to launch the strikes so desperately needed, because of the political ramifications. The United States had just come out of three bloody years of fighting in Korea, and was thus reluctant to commit its powerful carrier resources to aid the French.

With the fall of Dienbienphu on May 7, 1954, the French effort in Indochina suffered a strategic and political defeat. Public clamor at home forced the French government to actively seek a peace with the triumphant Vietminh. The Geneva Agreements of 1954 partitioned Vietnam into North and South Vietnam, with a Demilitarized Zone (DMZ) along the 17th parallel. But peace did not come to the region. The Communists continued their activities, conducting guerrilla warfare in the south. They also began infiltrating neighboring Laos to aid the rebel Pathet Lao forces seeking the overthrow of the royal family of Prince Souvanna Phouma, as well as that of Prince Norodom Sihanouk in Cambodia.

Throughout the late 1950s and early 1960s, American carriers maintained a presence in the South China Sea, merely patrolling the beat, while the turbulence ashore continued. The *Midway* (CVA-41) with Air Wing 2 aboard, was off Vietnam in February 1961, when the trouble in Laos threatened to boil over into a larger conflict. The F8U-1Es of VMF-312 were flying CAP missions as a

The aircraft carrier *Midway*, as she appeared in the early 1960s. One of three "large" carriers (CVB) completed just after World War II, she carries a standard air wing of the period: F8U Crusader and F3H Demon fighters, A4D Skyhawk and AD Skyraider attack planes, A3D Skywarrior "heavies," and early warning and "recce" aircraft, the last F8U-1P Photo Crusaders. (U.S. Navy)

precaution. When the Soviet Union hurriedly sent supplies to aid the Pathet Lao, the United States countered with six antiquated T-6 trainers to the royalist forces. The World War II trainers were to be used as fighter-bombers against the insurgents. When the Vietnamese Communists (now referred to as Viet Cong) sent troops to aid the Pathet Lao, the whole of Southeast Asia seemed ready to ignite. However, a coalition government was finally agreed upon including both Pathet Lao and royalist interests, and the trouble died down for the moment.

The United States decided in the interim to supply South Vietnam with aid packages including field advisers, communication equipment, arms, and aircraft. The situation seemed to be coming under

Unarmed reconnaissance aircraft had a major role in American participation in Vietnam. The first U.S. military aircraft used over Vietnam in the 1960s were reconnaissance aircraft, like this RF-8A (formerly F8U-1P) Photo Crusader from the *Midway*. Note the Crusader's distinctive "wing-up" configuration for landing, lowered hook and wheels; and camera openings under national insignia. (U.S. Navy)

control, enabling Secretary of Defense Robert S. McNamara to declare that American aid was beginning to work against the Communists. However, the South Vietnamese army was not up to fighting so strong an enemy as the Communists. Indeed, under the repressive regime of Ngo Dinh Diem, president of South Vietnam since 1954, the country was ripe for a step-up in Viet Cong activity.

On November 1, 1963, a coup overthrew the dictator and his family. Diem was murdered on the way to the headquarters of those generals who remained loyal. Another government was installed with General Duong Van Minh at its head, but by January 30, 1964, Minh had been overthrown by General Nguyen Khanh. General Khanh found himself facing daily demonstrations by disgruntled Buddhists clamoring for a greater voice in the government. To counter the restive mood of the country, Khanh called for a more aggressive stance against the North, and urged his countrymen to invade North Vietnam. He was supported by the magnetic chief of South Vietnam's air force, General Nguyen Cao Ky. Khanh was becoming an embarrassment to the United States, and as a peace offering, President Lyndon B. Johnson, who had assumed the presidency after President John F. Kennedy's assassination in November 1963 — three weeks after Diem's death — allowed contingency planning for attacks on the North to start.

THE FIRST AMERICAN MISSIONS

While events alternatively simmered and boiled over in the Vietnamese capitals, American carriers patrolled the coast, on station in case the situation warranted more drastic action. But, while offensive air strikes were only a possibility in the minds of the carrier men, unarmed reconnaissance flights were a matter of fact. Throughout the early 1960s, airborne reconnaissance was a means of monitoring Communist activities offering good, immediate results, while providing little cause for political objection from other major powers, such as Russia and China.

However, these early pre-Tonkin Gulf missions were not without their hazards. Several VFP-63 pilots were shot down as they flew across suspected areas of Communist concentration. Some were rescued; some were never seen again. In this early period, two important aircraft missions were linked: reconnaissance, and Search and Rescue (SAR) by helicopter. In these first days of combat, prior to official U.S. involvement, the first tentative steps towards quick rescue under intense fire were taken. Although helicopter-borne rescue had been used in the Korean War a decade earlier, the helicopter was still thought of as the patient guard, stationed off the ship during operations, ready to pluck the occasional hapless aviator from the sea when his plane failed him. But, it soon became clear that when the pilots knew that every possible effort would be made to rescue them, their morale would be strengthened and their fortitude increased. The best way to insure a man's value and capability in a combat environment was to provide him with the best SAR efforts — ones he could depend on should he go down.

Vought RF-8As had been used to get photographic coverage of areas of interest, especially in Laos. In May 1964, Lieutenant Charles F. Klusmann launched from the carrier *Kitty Hawk* (CVA-63) for a reconnaissance mission over Laos. His Crusader was hit by ground fire. Although the airplane burned for twenty minutes en route back to the carrier, Klusmann was able to bring his Crusader back safely.

However, two weeks later, on June 6 Klusmann's airplane was again hit by ground fire. This time, the damage was so severe that Klusmann had to eject near Communist troops. The Pathet Lao

The *Kitty Hawk* at sea. One of the *Forrestal*-class "super" carriers, she can operate up to ninety aircraft. In this photo a pair of 35-ton A-3B Skywarriors sit on her forward catapults, and a pair of F-4B Phantom fighters are on the two angled-deck catapults. Note the markings of the angled deck, which permit a plane missing an arresting wire to accelerate and take off for another landing run. (U.S. Navy)

forces immediately set out to capture the Navy pilot, firing on a rescue chopper sent to pick him up. The helicopter was finally forced to abandon Klusmann who, to make matters worse, had twisted his ankle during his parachute landing. The VFP-63 pilot was captured but after three months in captivity, managed to escape with several Laotian prisoners. After two days of hiding in the jungle from his captors, Klusmann was able to reach a government camp and was eventually rescued.

Although the rescue helicopter in this case was unable to get Klusmann, it was missions like this that laid the ground work for the efficient and relatively successful operation which SAR was to become. There were other aviators, such as Lieutenant Commander Harvey A. Eikel, who, after ejecting from his mortally wounded photobird, found himself ringed in by Communists, and was rescued by helicopter. The pilots knew that all the stops would be pulled out to get them, if they ejected.

In addition to the pre-1964 activities of the American air services, the Marines provided the first contingent of helicopters in April 1962. This was the beginning of Operation Shufly, which enlarged the troop and cargo life capability of the small South Vietnamese Army. Operating from Da Nang, the Shufly helos flew in support of the South Vietnamese. By December 1964, the operation was renamed Marine Unit Vietnam.

2

The Gulf of Tonkin

There were now ships of the U.S. Seventh Fleet passing off the Indochina coast on a routine basis, gathering intelligence, supporting anti-Communist activities, and launching recon flights. Thus it is no wonder that the Viet Cong and their allies betrayed their edginess with an attack that pushed the Americans into the forefront of the battle. The 2,200-ton destroyer *Maddox*'s radar detected the approach of three unidentified high-speed craft on the afternoon of August 2, 1964. The *Maddox* was passing off the coast of Hon Me Island, thirty miles south of the North Vietnamese PT-boat base at Loc Chao, which South Vietnamese commandos had raided the night before.

Identified as North Vietnamese torpedo boats, the onrushing targets headed straight for the *Maddox*, a warning shot failing to deter them. At a range of nearly three miles, two of the Communist

This photo, taken aboard the destroyer *Maddox* in the Gulf of Tonkin on August 2, 1964, shows a North Vietnamese torpedo boat under fire from the U.S. warship. A shell splash can just be seen in the PT-boat's wake. The PT-boat attack and one that followed two nights later led to U.S. carrier air strikes against their bases in North Vietnam. (U.S. Navy).

boats each fired a torpedo; both missed the *Maddox*, which had taken evasive action. The U.S. destroyer returned the fire, possibly hitting the third North Vietnamese boat.

While this engagement was in progress, a flight of four F-8E Crusaders of VF-53, previously launched from the *Ticonderoga* (CVA-14) on a training mission, was vectored to the area. Upon establishing contact with the *Maddox* and the embarked destroyer division commander, the Crusaders were ordered to attack the remaining PTs as they retired to the north. Armed with 20-mm cannon and Zuni unguided rockets, the Vought fighters swung in over the North Vietnamese craft, and made several strafing runs. In the opinion of the

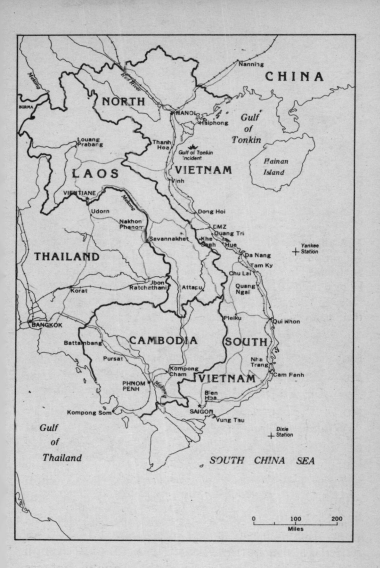

Crewmen aboard the carrier *Ticonderoga* load Zuni air-to-surface rockets aboard F-8 Crusaders as the ship prepares to launch fighters to fly cover for U.S. destroyers in the Gulf of Tonkin. Two 20-mm gun openings are visible just below the number "203," indicating the third aircraft of the second squadron aboard the carrier. (U.S. Navy)

flight leader, Commander R.F. Mohrhardt, who was also the commanding officer of the squadron, they sank the third torpedo boat. From the initial contact by *Maddox*'s radar to the retirement of the American destroyer after the sinking of one of the attackers, approximately three and a half hours had passed.

By presidential order, the *Maddox* was joined by the destroyer *Turner Joy*. The carrier *Constellation* (CVA-64) was also routed from Hong Kong to the Tonkin Gulf, some 400 miles away. Meanwhile the planes from *Ticonderoga* maintained a daylight watch; during the night, the destroyers would retire to about 100 miles offshore to reduce the danger of night torpedo-boat attack. But on the night of August 4 the *Maddox* picked up five high-speed contacts, identified as North Vietnamese torpedo boats about to make a nighttime run. In the bad weather which covered the area, the two forces exchanged ineffectual gunfire. Torpedoes from the PTs narrowly missed the destroyers. *Ticonderoga* launched two A-1 Skyraiders in an attempt to provide air cover, but by midnight the torpedo boats had vanished from the radar screens.

With two unprovoked attacks on American men-of-war in international waters now a reality, the time for retaliatory action had come. President Johnson went on television to announce the actions he intended to take. He had planned the American response carefully. Even as he spoke to the nation, detailing the events of recent days in the Tonkin Gulf, planes from *Constellation* and *Ticonderoga* were airborne and heading for four major PT-boat

The A-1 Skyraider or "Spad" was the last piston-engine fighter or attack plane to be flown from U.S. carriers. This A-1 is preparing to take off from the carrier *Hancock* with a load of light bombs and rocket pods. She will deck launch at the flight deck officer's signal, without the use of a catapult, the last U.S. combat aircraft with that capability. (U.S. Navy, Robert Moeser)

bases along the North Vietnamese coast. The area of coverage ranged from a small base at Quang Khe 50 miles north of the demarcation line between North and South Vietnam, to the large base at Hon Gai in the north.

Johnson said, "Our response for the present will be limited and fitting. . . . We still seek no wider war. . . ." His remarks had been in coordination with the ongoing attack half a world away. "That reply is given as I speak to you tonight. Air action is now in execution against gunboats and certain supporting facilities in North Vietnam which have been used in these hostile operations." F-8s, Skyhawks and Skyraiders bombed and rocketed the four bases, damaging all the facilities and destroying or damaging an estimated twenty-five PT boats, more than half of the North Vietnamese force. It was during these attacks that twenty-six-year-old Lieutenant (j.g.) Everett Alvarez from the *Constellation* was shot down in his A-4C over Hon Gai. He ejected and was captured by the North Vietnamese, becoming the first POW of the war. He walked out of confinement in 1973 after eight and a half years in prison.

Although the attack on the PT-boat bases was in direct response to the attacks in the Tonkin Gulf, there could be little doubt that the North Vietnamese were preparing or had already planned systematic violations, and therefore a contingency plan for further retaliatory strikes was needed. For the next six months after the Tonkin Gulf Incident, and with the passing of the Gulf of Tonkin Resolution by Congress on August 10, 1964, the men and ships of Task Force 77 stood by, prepared with various bombloads should an additional attack be required.

The full range of carrier aviation had been suddenly brought into play by the North Vietnamese attack on *Maddox* and *Joy*. The aircraft aboard the two carriers *Ticonderoga* and *Constellation* were immediately available for retaliatory strikes; their use required no negotiations with a third country for air bases, and no delay for permission to overfly a third country to carry out the attack mission. The United States acted entirely on its own, with no need to consult other nations.

However, the decision was made to take no chances. The attack carrier *Ranger* (CVA-61) and the ASW carrier *Kearsarge* (CVS-33) were detailed to steam towards the Tonkin Gulf, the *Ranger* to provide additional attack capability, and the *Kearsarge* to guard against any possible Communist Chinese submarine activity. This would give TF77 a striking force based on three attack carriers and one ASW carrier. The Communists shifted a few fighter units into North Vietnamese bases from Red China, but otherwise made no overt moves to counter the carrier force off shore. The United States, in turn, brought several Air Force units to South Vietnam, as well as support personnel and equipment. The buildup had begun.

BUILDUP AND FRUSTRATION

Americans had not been involved in a large-scale shooting war for almost twelve years. The experiences of Korea were beginning to fade and the prospect of American soldiers fighting and dying once again in a far-off Asian country was unsettling to most citizens listening to the President that midsummer's evening in August. But after the initial furor of the Tonkin Incident, the country heard little about the war. There were occasional newspaper reports of terrorist activities in Saigon and outlying countryside hamlets, and sometimes a news item telling about an aircraft carrier off the coast. But things were relatively quiet as far as the United States was concerned, until February 1965.

The *Hancock*, one of the extensively modernized *Essex* class (CV-9) carriers, was the smallest type of flattop to operate in the Vietnam War. Their air wings were limited in that they could not operate the larger F-4 Phantoms and A-6 Intruders when those aircraft became available. During a lull in flight operations the *Hancock*'s forward elevator is in the lowered position. (U.S. Navy, L.P. Bodine)

At that time, unrest in South Vietnam and dissatisfaction with General Khanh's government had led to street demonstrations and acts of terrorism by the Viet Cong. The United States sent an advisory team under National Security Advisor McGeorge Bundy to observe the situation and recommend appropriate planning.

On February 7, 1965, shortly before Bundy's team was to leave South Vietnam, the United States compound at Pleiku in the Central Highlands was attacked by Viet Cong guerrillas. Nine Americans were killed and a hundred wounded. To American

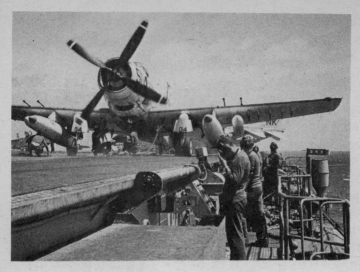

During the August 1964 combat operations by the carriers of Task Force 77, an A-1 Skyraider is hooked up to a catapult aboard the *Constellation*. The prop-driven "Spad" had a major role in the jet-age Vietnam War. This A-1 has the standard four 20-mm wing cannon and carries rocket pods and drop tanks on its wing pylons. (U.S. Navy, R.D. Moeser)

officials in South Vietnam, there seemed little choice but to make another strike in response to this latest outrage. President Johnson authorized a Navy strike, in concert with elements of the South Vietnamese Air Force, against the military barracks and staging area at Dong Hoi, north of the DMZ. Three other ships had entered the area: *Coral Sea* (CVA-43), *Ranger* and *Hancock* (CVA-19). The strike, which had been given the somewhat evocative title Flaming Dart I, was delayed by the inclement weather characteristic of the South China Sea at this time of year. However, the South Vietnamese contingent, led by no less a personage than General Ky, the air force commander, in his personal Douglas A-1H Skyraider, found a secondary target at Vinh.

By noontime, orders were given for the carriers to launch their aircraft, the *Coral Sea* and *Hancock* launching forty-nine aircraft directly against the barracks at Dong Hoi, and the *Ranger* sending a thirty-four plane force 15 miles inland against the barracks at Vit Thu Lu. The *Ranger*'s planes were unable to hit their designated target because of the weather, but the strike at Dong Hoi by *Coral Sea* and *Hancock* destroyed much of the facility. One A-4E from *Coral Sea* was lost, its pilot Lieutenant E.A. Dickson ejecting over the water. He was never found.

Settling back to assess the results of the strike at Dong Hoi and its effect on the political situation, the Americans knew that another response was due from the Communists. They had not long to wait. On February 10 the Viet Cong blasted an old hotel in Qui Nhon being used as an enlisted men's quarters, killing twenty-three American soldiers and wounding many more. Admiral U.S. Grant Sharp, Commander-in-Chief, Pacific, called for an immediate response. Flaming Dart II began the next day. The three aircraft carriers flew off another strike aimed at the Chanh Hoa barracks, 35 miles north of the DMZ. The ninety-nine aircraft in the strike force faced the same weather as the strike on February 7 — 500-foot ceilings and less than one-mile visibility. The northeast monsoon, as this system of rain and fog was technically called, was to plague the carrier fleet for the entire war. Only the advent of more technically capable aircraft, able to fly right through the scud and bomb accurately with little or no visual reference, would overcome the tremendous problems posed by the weather.

The shadow of an RF-8A Photo Crusader streaks over the water near a devastated North Vietnamese PT-boat during a raid on the torpedo boats' bases. Flying low and unarmed, the Photo Crusader provided both pre-strike and post-strike photography vital for mission planning and evaluation. (U.S. Navy)

44

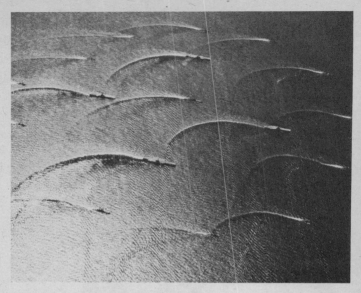

Carrier striking force in the South China Sea: the attack carriers *Coral Sea, Ranger*, and *Hancock*, plus the ASW carrier *Yorktown*, maneuver with a screen of cruisers and destroyers. Together they formed Task Force 77, the carrier striking force of the U.S. Seventh Fleet in the Western Pacific. In actual operations the ships rarely maneuvered this close together. (U.S. Navy)

The northeast monsoon is born with the surface winds which spread inland from the South China Sea from November through April. When the warmer air meets the cooler outbreaks of polar air pushing southward from Siberia and China, the system begins a clockwise swirl which produces northeasterly surface winds that reach from the South China Sea to continental Asia. The mountainous terrain of North Vietnam also contributes to the formation of this system of rain and clouds,

Weather would plague carrier operations throughout the Vietnam War. Here an F-8 Crusader from VF-211 is prepared for launching from the carrier *Bon Homme Richard* during a rainstorm in March of 1967. Although officially rated as a "day fighter," Crusaders often flew at night and in poor weather as evidenced by this launch in the South China Sea. (U.S. Navy, R.D. Moeser)

46

which was known as the "Crachin," to the Vietnamese and the sailors who plied the waters off Vietnam. The mountains block other air masses, and trap the cold air sweeping southward from continental Asia. The cooler air is funneled through the mountains, forcing itself against the warmer air from the sea, enlarging and strengthening the monsoon.

At any rate, the formidable monsoon seemed to be at its height during the early strikes of February 1965. The Flaming Dart strike of February 11 met with limited success as the aircraft from the *Ranger, Coral Sea*, and *Hancock* roared in against the Chanh Hoa barracks. The North Vietnamese responded with heavy antiaircraft fire, damaging a few American planes and shooting down three others. Two pilots were rescued, but the third man was captured after ejecting from his crippled F-8. These raids were the first of the so-called Alpha Strikes which included all available elements of the carrier's air wing, from fighters to tankers.

The F-8-equipped fighter squadrons at this time were tasked with various CAP (Combat Air Patrol) stations, such as TARCAP (Target CAP) and SARCAP (protection for the rescue aircraft). After the Gulf of Tonkin Incidents of August 1964, a standing air patrol, known as DeSoto Patrol CAP, was mounted. The DeSoto Patrols involved electronic intelligence gathering by ships eight to ten miles off the North Vietnamese coast. In addition to providing cover for the air strikes, the F-8 squadrons flew CAP for the ships engaged in DeSoto operations. The F-8s, fitted with limited air-intercept radar,

An aviation ordnanceman attaches a Sidewinder heat-seeking, air-to-air missile to an F-8 Crusader aboard the *Bon Homme Richard*. The Crusader was the principal U.S. naval fighter during the early Vietnam War, carrying missiles and bombs in addition to an internal gun armament. The F-4B Phantom, which replaced the Crusader aboard larger carriers, did not have a gun armament. (U.S. Navy, R.D. Moeser)

were armed with two to four Sidewinder air-to-air missiles, in addition to their 20-mm cannon with 400 total rounds, and Zuni rockets for flak suppression.

An interesting division within the F-8 mission also developed sometime later in early 1966. Some squadrons, such as VF-24, were equipped with F-8Cs, while others, such as VF-211, flew F-8Es. The E model with wing hardpoints had a heavier, reinforced wing which could carry extra Sidewinders or bombs. The Charlie carried only Sidewinders on fuselage racks. The Echoes, because of their extra weight, sometimes arrived back at the ship with less available fuel than desirable. The Cs, therefore, were allocated the actual CAP role, flying at higher altitudes, while the Echoes were used to attack ground targets.

The results of the Flaming Dart raids were inconclusive, especially the second strike. The Viet Cong were unimpressed by U.S. actions and continued their program of periodic terrorism against U.S. installations. It was becoming evident that a program of mere response to Communist acts was not going to have much of an effect. The President was

Most strikes from U.S. carriers against Vietnamese targets in the early stages of the war were flown by this duo: the A-1 Skyraider and A-4 Skyhawk, in this case from VA-152 and VA-163, respectively, both based aboard the *Oriskany*. Both aircraft have centerline "drop tanks" and the A-4 is also fitted with a standard in-flight refueling probe, extending from the starboard side of the fuselage. (U.S. Navy)

advised and gradually pressured to allow an ongoing program of interdictive strikes to begin.

3

The Air Campaign Against the North

Under the code name Rolling Thunder, the U.S. Air Force and Navy were tasked with bombing missions that were to progress from north of the DMZ to the outskirts of Hanoi. The Rolling Thunder concept was that as the bomb line moved nearer to the North Vietnamese city, the Communists would sue for peace when their capital was threatened.

Whatever promise the Rolling Thunder plan held was to be largely negated by high-level interference. To the consternation of most senior military commanders, Navy and Air Force, severe restrictions would be imposed on the missions. No strike was to be flown without prior administration approval. No pre-strike photography was permitted. Instead, the reconnaissance aircraft, the RF-8s of VFP-63, and the more sophisticated and expensive RA-5C Vigilantes, were either to accompany the strike force into the target area, or fly immediately after the bombers for bomb-damage assessment. (The recon-

This A-4 Skyhawk has just caught the No. 1 wire while coming aboard the carrier *Hancock* after a mission over North Vietnam. Barely visible under the aircraft's right wing is the plane guard destroyer, steaming in the carrier's wake to pick up the crew of any aircraft that "goes into the drink" during the flight operations. (U.S. Navy, R.D. Moeser)

naissance community was not pleased with this particular restriction. Many pilots and crews were lost or captured, along with their valuable aircraft and photography, because the North Vietnamese defenses were, of course, alerted by the time the main strike force had passed over the target, leaving the men on the ground ready and waiting for the lone RF-8 which they knew would be coming right behind.)

Another restriction placed on the Rolling Thunder missions was that no follow-up secondary strike could be authorized, thus eliminating the one-two-punch combination which is elementary to combat, whether the form is boxing or airborne strikes. Unexpended ordnance could not be used on a target of opportunity, but had to be dropped into the water prior to returning to the ship. As far as any air-to-air combat was concerned, the rule was laid down that enemy aircraft had to be positively identified before engaging—more easily said than done when closing speeds were on the order of 1,000 miles per hour. And to top the whole thing off,

Returning from a mission, a pair of F-8 Crusaders from the *Hancock*'s VF-211 lower their arresting hooks; in a short time their wheels will come down as they line up in the landing pattern to come aboard the carrier. The skills required for overwater navigation as well as carrier takeoffs and landings make naval aviators the world's best. (U.S. Navy)

should weather or operational considerations force cancellation of the mission for a particular day, the entire process of authorization had to be repeated prior to rescheduling.

As restrictive as the rules were, minor attempts were made to smooth things out—a bit. Specific targets were assigned to Navy and Air Force units, and then finally refined into designated "route packages," relieving some confusion. Two geographic points were selected in the Gulf of Tonkin, and designated Yankee and Dixie Stations, north and south, respectively. Originally Yankee Station was created to serve as a central location for operations against North Vietnam. Dixie Station was actually created some time later at the request of General William Westmoreland, Commander, U.S. Military Assistance Command, Vietnam. Westmoreland was so impressed by the Navy's carrier support of infantry operations that he asked for a permanent carrier presence off South Vietnam. This presence was all the more necessary because of a lack of proper land bases from which ground support aircraft could operate.

While Westmoreland's request was a feather in the cap of naval aviation, it also put a further burden on the carrier forces requiring ships to stay at sea much longer than the normal line period, servicing both stations. The Navy found it necessary by June 1965 to deploy no less than five attack carriers in the South China Sea to accomplish its tasks. Dixie Station also evolved into a sort of "warming up" area for newly arrived carrier air wings. In the relatively "peaceful" atmosphere of the southern war zone, where Communist air defense was at a minimum, green air crews could get their feet wet. They could get used to dropping bombs, to strafing running figures on the ground, and to the unrelenting pressure of daily combat operations before going north into the "real" world of AAA, missiles, MiGs and the threat of capture.

The first Navy strike of the Rolling Thunder program occurred on March 18, 1965, when aircraft from the *Coral Sea* and *Hancock* bombed supply buildings at Phu Van and Vinh Son, all of the aircraft returning with light damage. However, successive attacks brought increased casualties, aircraft losses, and capture. The attacks moved up and down the North Vietnamese coastline, coming within 70 miles of Hanoi. While the strikes seemed to do some strategic good, the main result was that the Communists stopped travelling and resupplying their units during the day. Instead they switched to small camouflaged activity at night along what was to become known as the Ho Chi Minh Trail, which eventually stretched from North Vietnam to Laos. People became one of the commonest means of transporting supplies, along with trucks. Because of a restriction against U.S. bombing of villages, the Viet Cong parked their vehicles in the open in broad daylight where they could be clearly seen, and therefore be safe from attack.

MARKET TIME OPERATIONS

In addition to the February and March air strikes of Flaming Dart and Rolling Thunder, other important operations were begun. In February, a maritime surveillance program was instituted in which air and surface units of both the U.S. Navy and Vietnamese forces patrolled the various rivers for waterborne Communist supply efforts. In company with "Swift" boats, various patrol squadrons—VP-4, VP-17, VP-40, to name a few—operated their P-2 Neptunes, and later P-3 Orions, as well as P-5 Marlins, the last flying boats used on operations by the United States Navy. This operation, with the code name Market Time, ranged from southern Cambodia up to the 17th parallel, between the two Vietnams. It was a dull, usually colorless operation which received little coverage in the press. The relatively slow and long-ranged patrol aircraft just didn't qualify for the headlines back home, but to the men of the patrol squadrons which deployed for many long months to Vietnam on Market Time duty, it was the most important job in the world. Initially P-2s shouldered much of the burden. The SP-2H Neptunes, the long-lived, twin-engined (some with jet engines for augmented power) patrol bombers from Lockheed which had been operational since the end of World War II. Most of the West Coast VP squadrons deployed to Vietnam at one time or another.

Actually, the Market Time operation consisted of three different missions: Yankee Station, Market Time and OSAP (ocean surveillance patrols). Yankee Station missions involved the Tonkin Gulf area, and were flown at night, usually at heights no greater than 800 feet, and more likely 400-500 feet. Yankee Station aircraft were looking for fast mov-

An SP-2H Neptune maritime patrol aircraft from VP-4 takes a close look at a junk off Vung Tau along the coast of South Vietnam. These aircraft, designed to seek out and attack enemy submarines, were most effective in Market Time operations. The Neptune was powered by two piston engines with two jet pods fitted for "burst" speed and takeoff. (U.S. Navy)

ing targets, such as PT boats and aircraft—which were of great concern to the surface ships steaming in the Gulf, especially at night—and for downed crews. They flew without lights to lessen the chances of being seen. But the hundreds of small boats which trafficked the waterways were always lit up with running lights and cooking fires, "like a city at night," as one pilot put it.

The later P-3A Orions, which relieved the P-2 in 1967, came equipped with a radar-altitude-hold device which, when engaged, acted like an automatic pilot, keeping the big aircraft at the desired height. The controls could be operated much like the steering wheel of a car, without concern for rudder coordination; a mere turn of the wheel would alter

An SP-2H Neptune taxies behind barbed wire at the airstrip at Cam Rahn Bay. Note that the starboard wingtip of this VP-4 aircraft has the standard fixed fuel tank with searchlights mounted in the forward section. The bulge visible under the fuselage is for AN/APS-20 surface search radar. (U.S. Navy, William M. Powers)

Vietnam marked the last operational use of seaplanes by the U.S. Navy. Here an SP-5B Marlin passes low over the Vietnamese coastline, seeking boats or junks that may be carrying men and arms into South Vietnam. "QE" on the T-shaped tail indicates VP-40. These flying boats were useful and graceful, but less capable and expensive to support in comparison with land-based patrol aircraft. (U.S. Navy)

course. However, after the loss of a plane and its crew when the hold device malfunctioned undetected by the pilot, large red flasher lights were installed on the instrument panel to alert the pilots in case of a problem.

Market Time missions involved nearly one-half of the entire operations. Of special interest were the large steel-hulled trawlers supplied by Communist China. These vessels could bring in large amounts of cargo, and also offered a good radar return. The smaller wooden sampans were the greatest problems, because of their construction which did not give a good "paint" and because the little boats also carried a lot of legal supplies as well as contraband. Only boarding by Swift boats and other patrol craft could determine the actual nature of the cargo.

OSAP missions, which were generally maritime surveillance, involved shadowing suspicious vessels, particularly Russian and Chinese ships. But, in the words of a P-3 pilot, these OSAP missions were "generally fruitless and boring."

Definitely not boring was the mission flown by Spangle 8, a P-3 Orion of VP-16 on January 27, 1967. Operating from Utapao, Thailand, Spangle 8 — "Spangle" being the squadron radio call sign — reported on station off Da Nang and established a three-engine loiter surveillance pattern. In this procedure one engine was shut down to conserve fuel, sometimes two, depending on the plane's overall weight and length of patrol.

At 0145, Spangle 8 was directed to an area south of Chu Lai, where small boats were thought to be beached, offloading cargo. Climbing to 3,500 feet, as dictated by squadron policy, the Orion informed the minesweeper directing the investigation of its arrival and that four small boats were indeed by the shore. Any doubt of the intent of the unknown craft was quickly removed when the P-3 began taking ground-fire hits. In a fortunate turn of events, the aircraft was hit in the deactivated engine, outside on the port wing. Fuel began to stream from the tanks; had the engine been operating, the hot exhaust would have ignited the fuel, started a fire, and probably would have resulted in

A P-38 Orion from Patrol Squadron (VP) 31 in flight over the Pacific. The four-engine aircraft could cruise on two engines. With long endurance, a large weapons capacity, advanced sensors, and pressurized cabins, the Orions marked a major improvement in maritime reconnaissance capabilities over their predecessors, the Neptune and Marlin. (U.S. Navy)

the loss of the airplane and its crew.

Because the P-3A's engine fuel tanks were isolated, and therefore fuel could not be transferred from one to the other, balance soon became a problem. Fighting the controls, the pilot, Lieutenant Commander Richard Knott, informed the minesweeper of his situation and of his intention to head for Da Nang. The P-3 made one more sweep of the beach to guide oncoming armed helicopters to the Viet Cong boats and then declared an emergency to Da Nang approach control. Cleared for a straight-in approach, the Orion made an uneventful landing. The courage and skill of Lieutenant Commander

Knott had saved the expensive patrol plane, as well as perhaps the lives of his eleven crewmen.

Market Time aircraft also assisted in rescue operations of surface craft, especially the Vietnamese junks which populated the coastal waterways. On September 19, 1966, a P-2 of VP-2 investigated a junk, which quickly displayed signs calling for help, "ingine broken," and "boat is accident, plaise save." The P-2 pilot radioed Vung Tau, southeast of Saigon, which contained a coastal surveillance center. The facility at Vung Tau dispatched a minesweeper which eventually rescued thirty-two Vietnamese crewmen aboard the disabled junk.

The seaplane tender *Salisbury Sound* (AV-13) supporting SP-5B flying boats at Cam Ranh Bay. Note the SP-5B resting on her fantail, hoisted aboard by the 30-ton-capacity cranes on the fantail and atop the ship's amidships hangar. These tenders were large ships, displacing over 15,000 tons full load, and manned by a crew of about one thousand. (U.S. Navy, R.D. Moeser)

But, for the most part, Market Time patrol missions were long affairs, usually 10-13 hours in duration, with pilots gaining hundreds of hours of flight time during a tour. But the crews were not forgotten. On Christmas Eve, 1966, some lucky Orion crews celebrated the holiday with homebaked pies and even a small tree in the plane's aft compartment, as they flew the long night.

Another important operation during this period was the landing of the Marines at Da Nang on March 8. In the first wartime amphibious landing since the early days of the Korean War, the 9th Marine Expeditionary Brigade, some 3,500 men, landed to reinforce the anti-Communist forces in the city. It was a prelude to other Marine operations, such as the June landing at Chu Lai.

With the gathering momentum of Rolling Thunder and the increasing frequency of American air strikes, it was only a matter of time before the North Vietnamese took stronger defense measures. On April 5 an RF-8A from the *Coral Sea* brought back photography of the first Surface-to-Air Missile (SAM) site to be positively identified. The site, 15 miles southeast of Hanoi, was of such great importance that the commander of Task Force 77, the collective name for the group of Navy ships off the Vietnamese coast, flew to Saigon to show the pictures to the commander of the 7th Air Force. Both men agreed that immediate action was required to meet this new and dangerous threat to American flight crews. A joint plan was forwarded up the chain of command for a Navy/Air Force strike at the missile site. But permission to mount such a strike was refused. A second site appeared a month later and by July several SAM sites were in evidence.

It was not until several American planes had been shot down—the first Navy losses were VA-23 A-4s from the *Midway* in August—that official sanction was given to anti-SAM missions. The operation, with one of the innumerable nicknames of the Vietnam War, Iron Hand, began on August 12, but although considerable effort, as well as men and material, was expended in hunting out sites, the first actual strike against a SAM site was not accomplished until the morning of October 17. Four A-4Es from the *Independence* (CVA-62), with an A-6 pathfinder, found a site near Kep airfield, north of Hanoi, and destroyed it. (The Air Force had its own methods for killing SAM sites in the "Wild Weasel" aircraft, initially two-seat F-105s equipped with electronic jamming devices.)

SAMs were not the only defensive measures undertaken by the North Vietnamese. Additional early-warning radar sites were installed as fast as possible, and a large infusion of aircraft could be seen as the months progressed, especially MiG-17s. The MiG-17 was an outgrowth of the Korean War-vintage MiG-15 which had given the Air Force such a scare in the early 1950s. Although much slower than the supersonic F-4s of the Navy and Air Force, which formed much of its opposition, the MiG-17 with greater maneuverability and cannon armament posed a very real threat to the American aviators. This was to say nothing of the threat posed by the more advanced MiG-21, an entirely different and

Barbed wire protects a flight line of P-3 Orions from VP-50 at Cam Ranh Bay in Vietnam. Land-based aircraft in South Vietnam and even Thailand were vulnerable to Communist guerrillas; aircraft aboard carriers were not vulnerable to this threat. (U.S. Navy, E.R. Ortiz)

faster aircraft which, the American commanders knew, would soon appear in the skies over North Vietnam.

With the SA-2 Guideline SAMs deployed in increasing numbers, the attacking aircraft were forced to fly lower, outside the missile's performance parameters, only to meet antiaircraft guns which, according to some of the older pilots who had also flown in World War II, were more intense and disruptive than any flak they had encountered over Germany twenty years earlier.

The introduction of surface-to-air missiles and radar-directed antiaircraft guns gave rise to a unique and sometimes costly little war-within-a-war, elec-

Crewmen aboard the carrier *Midway* wait for the next launch of an F-8 Crusader against targets in North Vietnam. Their momentary pause is caused by the cloud of steam coming from the catapult track. Different colored jerseys on the crewmen indicate their assignment — yellow for plane directors, blue for elevator operators and plane handlers, green for catapult and arresting gear personnel, brown for plane captains, red for ordnancemen and fire fighters, etc. (U.S. Navy, Karl Hedberg)

tronic countermeasures. The SA-2s used throughout the Vietnam War, and indeed in other areas of conflict, such as the Mideast, were usually described by the pilots fortunate enough to see them and return, as flying telephone poles. A 35-foot two-stage rocket with a 349-pound high explosive warhead and a ceiling of nearly 60,000 feet, the Guideline necessitated a whole new defensive system. SAM and flak suppression were obviously very high on the list of U.S. priorities as the war developed.

Against the concentrations of missiles along the various route packages flown by U.S. planes, each service developed its own attack methods and armaments. An early plan was to fly towards the target

An A-4E Skyhawk from the carrier *Independence* starts to pull up after an attack on railroad boxcars at Van Hoi in North Vietnam. This Skyhawk is using the Bullpup short-range missile. The boxcar at left was damaged in an earlier raid. (U.S. Navy)

at low level and high speed, until a pre-planned point of identification was reached, usually a prominent landmark, or bend in a river. At that time, the pilot would alter course to another pre-planned point, pull his plane into a climb, and then dive towards the target, release his ordnance and exit the area. There were several faults with this "pop-up" procedure, the most serious of which were that the low-level approach brought the bombers down to the range of small-arms fire, and that there was enormous pressure on the pilot to quickly identify

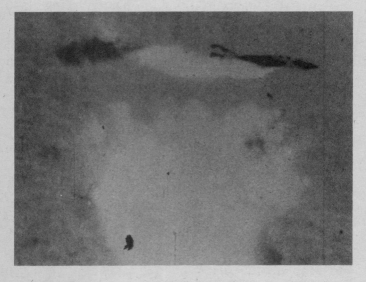

A North Vietnamese SA-2 missile explodes under an Air Force RF-4C reconnaissance aircraft near Hanoi. A stream of smoke has already begun to trail from the damaged Phantom. Few photos exist of such activity, as pilots in the heavy missile environment were too often busy maneuvering their aircraft. This shot was taken from the fighter escort flying wing for the unarmed recce aircraft. (U.S. Air Force)

his several landmarks and target accurately at high speed.

THE ELECTRONIC WAR

Other anti-SAM measures included use of chaff — countless strips of aluminum foil dropped prior to the strike. This oldest of electronic counter-measures, dating back to the Battle of Britain in 1940, was adequate, but the aircraft which carried and released the chaff had to fly tight formations at low levels to sew a proper pattern. Thus they needed their own armed escorts.

Air-launched missiles were also used against SAMs. The AGM-45A Shrike detected the North Vietnamese target-acquisition radar and homed onto the site, literally riding the beam down to impact. Although successful at first, the Communists countered the Shrike by alternatively turning their radar on and off, thereby reducing the time the signal was available for the Shrike to home on.

The Americans changed existing aircraft to meet the demands of SAM defense and detection. Most tactical aircraft such as the F-4 and the F-105 of the Air Force, could carry sophisticated jamming pods on their wing pylons, as well as missiles and bombs to drop on the sites once their location had been determined. The Navy used similar methods. Both services also employed larger aircraft which, while not being used in a strictly tactical sense, nevertheless served a very useful extension of their lives as electronic-warfare platforms. Two of the Navy aircraft in this category were the EA-3B Skywarrior and EF-10B Skyknight, older aircraft of the early 1950s.

The Skywarrior was the Navy's first all-jet bomber, originally developed as a nuclear-weapon delivery aircraft, and the largest aircraft to regularly operate from an aircraft carrier. However, with the Navy's airborne strategic delivery role taken over by the Air Force, the A-3, or A3D as it was known during its early service life, became a jack-of-all-trades: transport, tanker, and eventually an electronics and heavy photo-reconnaissance platform. (The Air Force used a development—not just a redesignated version—of the A-3, the EB-66C Destroyer, in much the same role.)

The Skyknight, actually older than the A-3, was a large twin-jet plane. Originally developed as a night fighter (and actually having claim to the first air-to-air night kill by a U.S. jet, in Korea), the big, old EF-10B was operated by Marines who affectionately called it the DRUT—the humor of which can be seen if the nickname is spelled backwards.

The EF-10B arrived at Da Nang on April 10, 1965 as a detachment of VMCJ-1, a Marine composite squadron tasked with varied duties, including reconnaissance and electronic intelligence. The unit initially provided the sole electronic-warfare capability for Air Force and Navy missions over the North. When the first Iron Hand anti-SAM strikes were flown by Air Force planes, the Marine EF-10Bs went along to give electronic support. No aircraft were lost to radar-controlled weapons during this strike.

The EF-10B soldiered on until 1969, finally giving

An A-4E Skyhawk of VA-72 in flight with two drop tanks and an AGM-12 Bullpup-A missile on its centerline pylon. The A model carried a 250-pound bomb as warhead and could be released up to seven miles from the target: the Bullpup-B carried a 1,000-pound bomb with slightly more range. An A-4 would carry up to three Bullpups. The missiles required the plane to continue to fly straight after launch to help guide the missile. (U.S. Navy)

way to the EA-6A Intruder which had more sophisticated electronics. However, prior to the arrival of the Intruders the EF-10s conducted continuous anti-SAM patrols along the DMZ after an A-4 was shot down by a SAM in April 1967.

THE FIRST AIR BATTLES

It was only a matter of time before air-to-air combat was joined between American flight crews and the Communist MiG pilots. The MiGs had actually made their first appearance during a fifty-plane U.S. raid south of Hanoi on April 3, 1965. The North Vietnamese fighters had made one firing pass at the strike force and had kept going. The next day, however, the MiGs' attention was a little more concentrated and the two first U.S. aircraft lost to enemy fighters were Air Force F-105s. In the following weeks, additional encounters occurred, but the Americans had yet to draw blood.

On June 17, Secretary of the Navy Paul H. Nitze was aboard the *Midway* as part of a tour of the fighting area. To his and the ship's delight, he had the opportunity to announce over the public address system that two VF-21 F-4B Phantoms had scored the first MiG kills of the war. The Executive Officer

Lieutenant (jg) Alan R. Crebo pilots his crippled A-4 Skyhawk back toward the carrier *Bon Homme Richard*. His nosewheel and hook are lowered, but his main wheels will not go down. This Skyhawk was damaged by antiaircraft fire over a Communist-held area of South Vietnam. (U.S. Navy)

of VF-21, Commander Louis C. Page, his Radar Intercept Officer, Lieutenant Jack E.D. Batson, Lieutenant John C. Smith, Jr., and Smith's RIO, Lieutenant Commander R.B. Doremus, had tangled with four MiG-17s south of Hanoi. As the two flights closed on each other at nearly 1,000 miles per hour, the two F-4s fired Sparrow missiles. Two MiGs burst into flames and went down.

On June 20, a third MiG-17 was brought down by a flight of VA-25 A-1 prop-driven Skyraiders, Lieutenant Clinton B. Johnson ultimately receiving credit for the kill. As the slower MiG used its maneuverability against the faster and less agile F-4s, so did the still slower A-1s use that same superior turning ability against the MiG. The United States was back in the game. Coincidentally, the *Midway*'s aircraft were also to score the final MiG kill of the war in 1973, some eight long years later.

An EF-10B Skyknight (formerly F3D-2Q) from Marine Composite Reconnaissance Squadron (VMCJ) 1 was one of the oldest aircraft used in combat in Vietnam. The Skyknights, modified from night fighters, were used for electronic surveillance and intelligence.

73

An EKA-3B Skywarrior of Airborne Early Warning Squadron (VAW) 13 from the carrier *Constellation* swings out over the Gulf of Tonkin. Note the electronic "blisters" or fairings along the plane's fuselage. Generally called "Whales," the Skywarriors served extensively in the electronic, tanker, and reconnaissance roles during the war, as well as serving — on a limited basis — as strike aircraft. (U.S. Navy, Paul R. Derby)

The Phantom was unquestionably the best fighter aircraft of the 1960s. This F-4B variant, armed with Sidewinder air-to-air missiles, is from VF-143 aboard the *Constellation*. The "00" or "double nut" marking indicates that it is flown by the air wing commander — always called "CAG" for air group commander despite the redesignation as carrier wings in 1962. (U.S. Navy)

SUPPORTING THE MISSION

The Marines had had plenty to do since their amphibious landing at Da Nang on March 8. Viet Cong sapper attacks were a constant threat to all U.S. and South Vietnamese installations, and the Communists seemed to single out supposedly protected aircraft for special attention with rocket and mortar fire. The regular Marine on the ground also needed help from his airborne brother Leathernecks. The establishment of an in-country Marine air base was a top priority.

Accordingly, in May 7, 1965, 1,400 Marines and Navy Seabees waded ashore at Chu Lai, some fifty miles south of Da Nang, to build an airfield expressly for ground-support operations. The landing was led by Brigadier General Marion Carl, the famed World War II fighter ace. By June 1, Chu Lai airstrip was declared operational and the A-4s of VMA-225 and VMA-311 flew the first missions against the Viet Cong. Even with a temporary bombing halt which had been offered as a peace overture on May 12, the Communists showed no signs of coming to the peace table, and, along with the resumption of other strikes, Marine aviation began to take on more responsibility with the opening of Chu Lai.

The diminutive A-4Es used by the Marines at Chu Lai operated from an innovative setup which was, essentially, a land-based aircraft carrier. Designated Short Airfield for Tactical Support or SATS, the airstrip employed a catapult and arresting gear, just like a carrier. Although the catapults were not

An F-8E Crusader of UMF (AW)-235 takes off from Da Nang in April 1967 for a close air support mission. (USMC)

Armed with rocket pods (lead plane) and bombs, A-4E Sky-hawks of Marine Attack Squadron (VMA) 223 taxi for takeoff at Chu Lai. Note that the lead plane's canopy is still open; centerline fuel tanks are fitted to both planes. (U.S. Navy, Robert L. Lawson)

Marine F-4Bs of UMFA-542 taxi prior to a mission from Da Nang. Some missions were also flown against the North by Marine Phantoms. (Dave Seder)

Marine UH-34 helicopters (Sikorsky S-58) take off from the helicopter carrier *Princeton* (LPH-5) during operations off Chu Lai. Operating from amphibious ships and shore bases, Marine helicopters were invaluable to American operations in Vietnam. (U.S. Navy, P.E. Huckans)

Marine ordnancemen fuse 250-pound Mk-81 bombs aboard attack aircraft at a South Vietnam airfield. The bombs have folding fins that extend after release. (U.S. Marine Corps, C. Stallings)

actually installed until 1967, heavier takeoffs were accomplished with the use of Jet Assisted Takeoff (JATO). The STATS-operational Chu Lai airstrip enabled A-4s to take off with a maximum bomb load in 3,600 feet.

Chu Lai also served as a main base of operations for helicopters. On the night of Friday, August 13, 1965, twenty-two UH-34Ds from HMM-361 and HMM-261 lifted off in waves of ten and formed up in column of twos to trap a suspected group of fifty Viet Cong using villages ten miles northeast of Da Nang as rest stops during the night. As the main helo force approached the landing zone, artillery softened up the surrounding terrain. Just before the touchdown, four armed Huey UH-1s from VMO-2 made several quick runs over the LZ to check for any last-minute danger. With flames dropped from a waiting Air Force transport, the UH-34s landed their troops. The operation netted several VC sympathizers and arms, including grenades and a rocket launcher.

Obviously the Marine airfield had to be destroyed, so the Viet Cong made plans to encircle the installation. By mid-August the Viet Cong's 1st Regiment had surrounded Chu Lai with about 3,000 troops. The Marines put Operation Starlight into action on August 18 to relieve the situation. In six days of heavy fighting, the VC received one of its first major defeats at the hands of the Americans. Billed as the largest Marine Corps operations in Vietnam history, Starlight involved elements of three Marine infantry battalions, five helicopter squadrons from land-based and ship-based units, as well as five fixed-wing jet squadrons from Marine Air Groups 11 and 12, flying Phantoms and Skyhawks respectively. The F-4s and A-4s alternated on station above the Van Tuong Peninsula day and night, covering the fight, hitting targets within 20-foot areas, while the Marines in the helicopters and on the ground bottled up the VC regiment, leaving little chance for escape. With the battle only 12 miles from the airfield at Chu Lai, Skyhawks took off with bombs and, like their Marine forebears twenty years before in Vought F4U Corsairs, dropped their ordnance before they could raise their wheels.

Operation Starlight cost the Communists over 600 men killed, in addition to loss of weapons. The Marines lost 50 men. Chu Lai had held, and provided support for Marine and Navy operations right up to the end of the American participation in 1973.

4

The New Air War

A major new aircraft entered the combat arena in June 1965, as the carrier *Independence*, on loan from the Atlantic fleet, steamed into the Gulf of Tonkin with VA-75 aboard. The "Sunday Punchers" had just finished working up with the A-6A Intruder, a state-of-the-art attack bomber which was to take the place of the A-3B as the "heavy" carrier-based weapons delivery system. Experiences in the Korean War, with the first use of carrier jets, had shown the definite need for a truly all-weather aircraft, capable of flying long distances, day or night, and delivering a load which made the effort worthwhile.

The prop-driven A-1 and later jet A-4 were obviously very satisfactory in their roles, but they were essentially clear-weather airplanes; pilot courage and skill could not always be trusted to get to the target through heavy rain in the dark of night. By

A-6A Intruders from the carrier *Constellation* set off on a bombing mission. These VA-156 aircraft show the Intruder's awkward appearance: thick forward fuselage with side-by-side seating for the pilot and, slightly behind him to his right, the bombardier/navigator; the narrow tail; and the refueling probe projecting up just forward of the cockpit. (U.S. Navy)

late 1960, the A-6A, or A2F as it was originally designated, completed its first flight, and two years later, in February 1963, VA-42 took delivery of the first production Intruders. The "Green Pawns" thus served as the training squadron for the A-6s.

A singularly unattractive airplane, which has been described variously as a frying pan, or a tadpole, the twin-engined A-6 employed the latest in "black box" weapon-delivery systems. The plane's mission required two crew members, the pilot and the bombardier/navigator, or B/N. Seated side by

The largest warship built until the mid-1970s, the nuclear-propelled carrier *Enterprise* is shown here with more than fifty aircraft on her flight deck. Her air wing consisted of more than ninety aircraft. Note the ship's squared-off "island" structure; the white panels are fixed-antenna AN/SPS-32/33 radars, with the island dome studded with electronic antennas. (U.S. Navy, L.N. Wilson)

side, the crew functioned as a coordinated team. The B/N used several futuristic devices to accurately target and deliver his bombs; the basis of these devices was the Digital Integrated Attack and Navigational Equipment, or DIANE. DIANE utilized several subsystems which together computed navigational, instrumentation, and situational information to give proper weapons delivery.

When the VA-75 Intruders launched from the *Independence* on July 1965, a lot of doubts and uncertainty rode with them. Could the multimillion-dollar aircraft with its fantastically complex and expensive computer system do its job? The answer

These A-6A Intruders from VA-196 aboard the carrier *Constellation* are en route to targets in Vietnam. The dark panels on the sides, under the "Navy" markings, are extending dive brakes. (U.S. Navy)

was an emphatic *yes*. From the beginning, although there were the usual bugs to be worked out, the A-6 showed its capabilities. That first mission took the new aircraft to targets south of Hanoi, the targets being located entirely by radar for the first time.

In the succeeding weeks, VA-75 took their aircraft against bridges, power plants, barracks, ammunition depots and railway installations in a continuous pounding of North Vietnamese territory, in every type of weather, fair or foul, day or night.

November saw the arrival of the *Kitty Hawk* with the second A-6 squadron, the "Black Falcons" of VA-85. Having recently transitioned from the trusty Skyraider, the new squadron took over where VA-75 left off, ranging up and down the South China Sea, from Dixie to Yankee Station and back again, using low-level approaches at high speed to escape enemy detection.

The impact of the Intruder upon the North Vietnamese was significant. Some measure of the effectiveness of the new airplane can be gained by a Radio Hanoi broadcast on April 20, 1966, some months later, when the North Vietnamese hotly claimed that the Americans were using B-52 heavy bombers against the population centers of the country. The proof, according to the Communist broadcaster, was the use of Stratofortresses against the Uong Bi power plant two days before. In truth, the strike against this important facility was accomplished by *two* Intruders of VA-85. Moreover, with the introduction of the A-6A, the Navy had conquered, or at least come to terms with, the monsoon and its adverse effect on flight operations in the Tonkin Gulf.

In November, the *Kitty Hawk*, along with the second contingent of A-6s, also brought another new aircraft to the hostilities, the E-2A Hawkeye from Grumman, the same company that made the Intruder. The Hawkeye was also a strange-looking airplane, with twin turboprop engines, four vertical stabilizers (three of which were actually necessary for controlled flight, the remaining surface being added for appearance's sake), and a large 24-foot-diameter radome which rotated at six revolutions per minute, on a pylon directly above the fuselage.

An E-2A Hawkeye lands aboard the carrier *Constellation* in the South China Sea. In the foreground the landing signal officer (LSO) uses instruments and a telephone in place of the twin paddles used by his predecessors in World War II. Note the aircraft's large turboprop engines, four-fin tail, and distinctive rotating radome. (U.S. Navy, Robert K. Drudge)

Although the *Enterprise* can operate for several years without refueling, her aircraft require constant replenishment of fuel and ordnance. Here the ammunition ship *Shasta* (AE-6) prepares to transfer munitions to the carrier. All four deck-edge elevators are lowered to the carrier's hangar deck. (U.S. Navy)

The E-2A mission was airborne early warning, vectoring fighters and strike bombers to and from targets on the ground, as well as airborne threats of MiG interceptors. A secondary role during combat operations was to relay message traffic from a strike force over its target to the carrier task force. Other uses were general surveillance, coordination of airborne refueling, vectoring aircraft in need of fuel to a waiting tanker, and search and rescue control. With a crew of two pilots and three or four systems operators, the Hawkeye was literally the aerial nerve center of the fleet, controlling bomber strikes and MiG-killing missions with equal facility.

ENTER NUCLEAR PROPULSION

By the end of 1965, all the major aircraft which were to continually operate during the Vietnam War, with the exception of the Vought A-7 Corsair II, were in place, and had made at least two combat deployments in respective carriers. The last major addition to the combat force was to appear on December 2, when the nuclear aircraft carrier *Enterprise* (CVAN-65) arrived on Yankee Station with Air Wing 9 aboard. Nuclear power had come to the war.

The largest warship ever built until that time, the *Enterprise* also included among her capabilities an Integrated Operational Intelligence Center (IOIC). This newest concept in intelligence was directly linked to the RA-5C Vigilantes of RVAH-7. The RA-5C was the definitive version of the earlier A-

The fuselage of the E-2 Hawkeye is crammed with electronic equipment plus displays for three operators. The cockpits, for pilot and copilot, are beyond the doorway at right. In the Airborne Early Warning (AEW) role the Hawkeye can detect hostile aircraft and direct friendly fighter or attack planes. (Grumman)

5A bomber developed during the very late fifties. The Mach 2 airplane was to employ a novel delivery system; it ejected its nuclear weapon out the rear of the plane, through a tunnel between its two engines.

The Vigilante had many developmental and operational problems in its early career, and by 1965 all of the bombers had been modified to RA-5C reconnaissance aircraft. The North American production line was then building only the C. The theory behind the multimillion-dollar reconnaissance plane and the IOIC was to centralize all the intelligence information gathered by the Vigilante, photographic

En route to Vietnam, the nuclear-propelled carrier *Enterprise* passes the carrier *Independence* in the Indian Ocean on November 21, 1965. The *Independence* was based at Norfolk, Virginia, and had just completed a deployment to Southeast Asian waters. (U.S. Navy)

as well as electronic, within a single area for developing, interpretation and dissemination to the fleet.

Enterprise carried a large component of warplanes, two F-4B fighter squadrons (VFs 92 and 96), four A-4C squadrons (VAs 36, 76, 93 and 94), "Heavy Seven" RVAH-7 with its Vigilantes, as well as another "heavy" squadron, VAH-4, which provided airborne refueling services with its KA-3Bs. There were also detachments of VAW-11, with E-1B Tracers, a plane whose role was an earlier version of the Hawkeye; HC-1 with UH-2 helicopters for SAR and utility duties; VAP-61 with RA-3Bs, although these generally operated from land bases; and the EA-3B of VQ-1, an electronic intelligence gathering platform.

The *Enterprise* brought a combination of the

newest technology and its own imposing physical presence to the Tonkin Gulf. After an initial workup on Dixie Station, the nuclear carrier had arrived on Yankee Station and on December 17, launched her first strike against targets in the north. By the end of her first week of combat operations, *Enterprise* had set a record of 165 combat sorties in one day, surpassing the *Kitty Hawk*'s 131. *Enterprise*'s commanding officer, Captain (later Admiral and Chief of Naval Operations) James L. Holloway III, commented, "The tons of bombs that have flown off this ship would stagger you."

A "Viggie" with hook and wheels down, and flaps extended, roars in for a landing aboard a carrier. The openings for cameras in the sensor pod are visible just behind the nosewheel. (U.S. Navy)

This is the modernized *Essex*-class carrier *Intrepid* while operating as a "limited" attack carrier on Dixie Station off South Vietnam. Some of the carriers participating in the Vietnam conflict were the veterans of three wars — World War II, Korea, and Vietnam, plus several major Cold War operations. Here the *Intrepid* has A-1 Skyraiders and A-4 Skyhawks parked forward, with an SH-3 Sea King helicopter aft on the starboard deck-edge elevator. (U.S. Navy)

The three carriers on station at the close of 1965 — *Enterprise, Kitty Hawk* and *Ticonderoga* — wound up the year with one of the biggest strikes yet thrown against the North Vietnamese. On December 22, 100 planes hit the thermal power plant at Uong Bi for the first time, the first time that an industrial target, as opposed to bases and support installations, had been sought. The large plant, a source of national pride for North Vietnam, was approached from the north by the planes from the *Enterprise*, while the *Kitty Hawk* and *Ticonderoga* force attacked from the south. By 1600, when the last wave of aircraft left the target, some 15 miles northeast of the harbor city of Haiphong, the plant was billowing forth oily smoke; all sections of the complex had been hit. Two *Enterprise* A-4s had been lost to the intense flak.

To the south, on Dixie Station, the antisubmarine carrier *Intrepid* (CVS-11) had been operating since May, in response to General Westmoreland's request for a carrier to support operations in South Vietnam. Originally an Atlantic fleet CVS, the *Intrepid*'s role had been changed in October to a "limited attack carrier," when she exchanged her S-2 Trackers, SH-3 helicopters and E-1 Tracers for twenty-eight A-4C Skyhawks and twenty-four Skyraiders.

By the time a Christmas truce was instituted on December 24, ten carriers had participated in combat action against the Communists since August 1964, and now many of them rotated home — first the *Coral Sea,* then *Midway, Independence, Bon Homme Richard* (CVA-31) and *Oriskany* (CVA-34). *Enterprise* and *Kitty Hawk* were left to carry on. In this first full year of the war, nearly 57,000 combat sorties had been flown from the carriers, with over 100 aircraft lost, eighty-two men killed, captured, or missing. Forty-six had been rescued.

However, when all these cold figures were totaled, and displayed for public and official consumption, the simple truth was that the Communists were not deterred in the least. Indeed, they were escalating the war. Rolling Thunder, the bombing program of intimidation, aimed at bringing the North to the peace table, was failing. The Viet Cong showed no signs of wanting to talk. But for now, it was too early to call the game off, and in an ever-present paradoxical situation, the carriers had proven their worth. Constantly under attack by critics as being too expensive, too vulnerable to attack, the giant ships that were really tiny airfields had carried the war to the enemy, and had supported their comrades on the ground in all types of conditions.

1966: HARD COMBAT BEGINS

The Christmas truce of 1965 and accompanying halt in bombing operations by the U.S. forces lasted for 37 days, while Washington waited in forlorn hope that the Communists would talk peace. But instead of responding, the North used the time to reconstruct bridges and facilities damaged in previous strikes, and to augment their growing air-defense network. Reconnaissance flights during the period gave ample evidence of the industry of the Viet Cong. Additional antiaircraft gun emplacements were disclosed between Hanoi and China's borders. Petroleum and lubricants facilities were being constructed underground to escape the next strikes. The Johnson Administration had to face the sobering and disheartening fact that the efforts of the previous year had been in vain. Rolling Thunder, Phase I, had been a dismal failure in its main objective, bringing the Communists around. The men and aircraft lost during the 1965 strikes had been wasted.

Secretary McNamara, speaking before Congress on February 23, 1966, however, spoke glowingly of the record and need for more carriers. With the *Midway* slated to be decommissioned for a while during a yard period of modernization, McNamara envisioned a fifteen-carrier fleet, using four nuclear-powered ships and eleven conventionally powered vessels.

Meanwhile Admiral Sharp, Commander-in-Chief, Pacific, pressed for resumed bombing operations against North Vietnam, saying ". . . a properly oriented bombing effort could either bring the enemy to the conference table or cause the insurgency to wither from lack of support." The administration, bowing to the concentrated pressure from senior military officials, gave the go-ahead for the resumption of attacks, but still retained some of the same restrictions which had been a hindrance during the previous year's operations: avoidance of foreign ships, MiG airfields, and large industrial targets north of Hanoi. A gradual change in policy was noticeable, however, as the strikes seemed to shift from purely retaliatory "punishment" raids to interdictive attacks against the flow of men and supplies to the front.

The monsoon was in full strength during the first part of the year, creating the normal restrictive weather patterns in the South China Sea, and directly affecting flight operations. The *Enterprise*, after a rest period in Subic Bay, Philippines, arrived on Dixie Station, with orders to hit enemy concentrations near the DMZ for nearly three weeks. Coming north to Yankee Station, March 17, the nuclear carrier and CVW-9, her air wing, flew strikes for a twenty-seven day period, at the height

An A-1H Skyraider with rocket pods taxies on the deck of the *Intrepid*. This is a single-seat "straight" attack version of the "Spad." A Skyraider from this squadron—VA-176—downed a MiG in the Vietnam air war, as did another A-1 from VA-25. Note the VA-176 bumblebee marking on the fuselage. (U.S. Navy, J.A. Bahrs)

of the monsoon.

Enterprise finally left the combat zone for Alameda, California, her home port (which she had yet to see), arriving there on June 21, 1966. The sight of the huge ship entering San Francisco Bay for the first time backed up traffic on the Golden Gate Bridge for twelve miles. Huge banners welcoming home the "Big E" were in abundance as were speeches and welcoming honors. During her first combat cruise, which had begun in December 1965, the *Enterprise* and her air wing had flown over 13,000 combat sorties, dropping nearly 9,000 tons of ordnance, and accumulating 18,142 arrested landings. But this record had not been achieved without cost.

A LONG HARD WAR

The redoubling of the Communists' air-defense system was proving a real threat; in January six aircraft and five crewmen were lost during raids; in February, ten planes and ten men went down. Flak seemed to be the greatest danger. SAMs, though in abundance, took a lesser toll. By October 1966, figures were published which indicated that of the 397 aircraft which had been lost, only 22 could be attributed to missiles. Of course, these figures were of little comfort to the crews who were captured or had to eject from their crippled planes after taking a hit from a SAM. Pilots discovered that avoidance of SAMs took courage, skill, and physical stamina. But the missile could be beaten. The tactic was devised wherein, the pilot, upon sighting the missile, would time himself and at the appropriate time (which only he himself, alone in his plane could judge) would execute a high-g turn counter to the missile's flight path. The missile's sensors would supposedly lose the target, breaking lock, and would eventually blow up without damage to its intended victim. The plan worked on a number of occasions, but it took iron nerve and resolve for a pilot to hold his plane steady until he pulled the stick hard over.

During the early months of 1966, there were rumblings of a serious problem affecting the entire

Several paint schemes were tried in Vietnam to reduce the vulnerability of low-flying attack aircraft. This green camouflaged A-4C Skyhawk is taxiing forward on the carrier *Enterprise* amidst conventionally painted aircraft, after a strike against North Vietnam. The tail code NG indicates Carrier Air Wing (CVW) 9, aboard for the "Big E" debut off Vietnam. (U.S. Navy, J.F. Falk)

military system, and especially the combat forces in Southeast Asia. By the time media representatives got wind of the situation, the services were well aware that there were serious shortages in everything from personal survival equipment to pilots themselves. In a front-page story on October 9, 1966, the *New York Times* pinpointed several areas of concern. Production was not keeping pace with combat attrition, even though the Secretary of Defense had authorized increased production; the combat loss rate was escalating, due to the commitment of increasing numbers of service squadrons to the fighting; the North Vietnamese had begun equipping themselves with a fearsome network of radar-directed guns and missiles.

As far as personnel were concerned, the paper quoted Representative Otis G. Pike, the Democratic chairman of a House Armed Services subcommittee on aircraft production and requirements, as saying that the Department of Defense had wasted too much time studying the problem. The proper solutions were increased production and training. Another source told of shortages of 1,660 Navy pilots and 650 Marine aviators. Competition from the commercial market, especially from the lucrative airlines, and frustration over government restrictions on the fighting, were cited as causes for the shortages in the cockpits.

Naturally concerned about its pilot and flight crew situation, the U.S. military made several recommendations and changes in this area. A Department of Defense investigation had shown that pilots were flying an average of between sixteen and

Ships and aircraft require fuels in considerable amounts. Every few days carriers on the line off Vietnam were replenished from fleet oilers, like the *Chipola* (AO-63), shown here refueling the *Ticonderoga* in heaving seas off the coast of Vietnam. During this particular operation the "Tico" took aboard 175,000 gallons of black oil for the ship's eight steam-producing boilers. (U.S. Navy)

twenty-two combat missions per month over the North, with some going as high as twenty-eight. Somewhere in this high rate of exposure, the odds were bound to narrow for many individuals, and the chance of going down increased tremendously. Therefore, Defense decided, no pilot could fly more than two complete deployments in a fourteen-month period. (This would help, but by war's end, in 1973, there were individuals who had flown over 500 missions, even with this restriction.) The training input for pilots was increased, but it would be eighteen months—the normal period during which a pilot entered the military community, studied military and aeronautical subjects, put in several hundred hours of flying as a student, and then gained his wings—before any improvement would be seen. To ease the immediate situation, some shore billets were eliminated and input to such "plum" assignments as postgraduate school was reduced. As training of crews was increased, so was the rate of manufacture of expendable ordnance, ammunition, and bombs. Stockpiles of World War II bombs were funneled into the pipeline, and a system of control and supply was initiated.

March saw the monsoon begin to abate slightly, and the hard-pressed crews of the strike groups welcomed the slightly clearer weather. This time also saw an interesting, if oddball, experiment in camouflage. CVW-11, operating from the *Kitty Hawk*, was ordered to repaint half of its aircraft in green camouflage paint, to render the planes less visible from above during operations. The Air Force had begun painting its planes in camouflage some months before, and the Navy thought an experiment might be useful. Accordingly, five squadrons of CVW-11 complied with the order: VA-85, flying A6As, VAs-113 and 115, flying A-4Cs, and RVAH-13, using RA-5Cs. The fifth squadron was unique for another reason as well. VF-213, the Black Lions, were flying a little-known version of the workhorse F-4 Phantom.

The F-4, perhaps the greatest and most ubiquitous of postwar American aircraft, started life as a

Two F-4B Phantom IIs of VF-114 fly toward their target in North Vietnam in April, 1967. The F-4 was unquestionably the best fighter aircraft of the 1960s. (U.S. Navy)

single-seat strike aircraft with a U.S. Navy requirement issued in September 1953. The requirements were refined through several years until August 1956, when work commenced on the prototype, then designated XF4H-1. By the time the new McDonnell jet had had its first flight on May 27, 1958, it had become a two-seat, highly advanced fighter capable of routinely reaching Mach 2.

Initially equipping Navy and Marine squadrons, the Phantom was paid the high compliment of being forced on the Air Force by Secretary McNamara as the F-110, for use as a strategic interceptor and strike fighter. Phantoms equipped major portions of the U.S. inventory and when the production line of F-4Bs, the first major production version, closed in 1966, 635 F-4s had come off the lines, with more to come. By 1978, when F-4 production finally ended, 5,211 aircraft had been manufactured, a post-World War II record, second only to production of the Air Force's F-86 Sabre series of over 5,400.

The F-4 was produced in several versions, some being reworks of existing models, the F-4Ns being updated Bs, and the F-4Ss being F-4Js with modifications for further service life. The aircraft equipped the air arms of many other countries as well as those of the United States, and the number was growing even at this writing.

One of the least used versions of the F-4, however, was the G model, ten of which found themselves as part of VF-213 on the *Kitty Hawk* in the South China Sea in the early days of 1966. Externally, the G was little different from the more

An A-6A Intruder from VA-85 in camouflage paint on the flight deck of the *Kitty Hawk* in April of 1966. The plane, with side number 807, has just landed aboard. Note the small national insignia ("stars-and-bars") and the "07" on the tail. Less visible is the aircraft's Bureau number (151787) and words "Navy" on either side of the fuselage. The light underside of the aircraft will blend with a clear sky while the dark overside will make spotting it more difficult to a MiG pilot when it flies low over the Vietnamese jungles. (U.S. Navy)

The F-4 Phantom was one of the most versatile aircraft of the Vietnam War. Here a Marine F-4B from VMFA-115 streaks toward a target, carrying twenty-four Mk-81 250-pound bombs. Although designed for carrier operation from the outset, it has been successfully used by the United States and several foreign air forces from land bases. (U.S. Navy)

prominent B. The difference was mainly due to a two-way data link system installed behind the rear cockpit, which would relay information from the carrier concerning mission requirements. The system was titled the RCA AN/ASW-21, and it also allowed the plane to fly a "hands-off" approach to the carrier. The data link system paved the way for other advanced electronics which found their way into other aircraft.

VF-213 operated its ten F-4Gs and two F-4Bs along with the F-4Bs of VF-114, the Aardvarks, through an intense period of combat. With the order to camouflage its aircraft, along with those of other squadrons of CVW-11, the squadron painted its Phantoms a thick matte green, as well as altering the various warning and informational signs scattered over the external surfaces. The national star-and-bar insignia was considerably reduced in size and squadron markings, except the air-group letters on the tail, were eliminated.

The camouflage was carried for the remainder of the cruise, into June. But the results were negative. During night operations, the dark green made the planes harder to see, and carrier operations at night, especially on a dark, rainswept deck, were dangerous at best, requiring the most visibility available. The Navy decided, upon the *Kitty Hawk*'s return to the States in June 1966, to eliminate the camouflage. But the episode had provided an interesting variation in color schemes.

The improving weather in March and April brought increased missions and increased loss rates. April was the most costly month to date, with twenty-one carrier aircraft and fifteen crewmen lost. The policy shift was becoming more evident as the action centered around the more industrialized areas of the North, especially the Vinh-Ben Thuy complex. On April 18, two A-6s from VA-85 struck the Uong Bi thermal power plant for the second time in the action mentioned above.

Since the first large strike on December 22, 1965, the power plant had been repaired. The complex supplied one-third of the power for Hanoi, and almost all for Haiphong. The two Intruders were launched from *Kitty Hawk* before midnight with the Commanding Officer, Commander Ronald J. Hays, of VA-85 and his B/N, Lieutenant Ted Been, and a second crew in the other aircraft. Armed with 13,000 pounds of bombs each, the two planes made their way to their target, racing along at low level to avoid radar detection. Updating their computers, the two made landfall as scheduled and attacked the target separately, within seconds of each other. The strike was so perfectly coordinated and executed that the North Vietnamese defenses were caught flat-footed. The A-6s had sped away before the guns on the ground opened fire. The twenty-six 1,000-pound bombs all hit the target, decimating the important complex. As mentioned before, the Communists were enraged and claimed that the Americans were using giant B-52 bombers against harmless civilian population centers.

A diplomatic incident occurred the next day, the 19th, when twenty-four aircraft from the *Kitty Hawk* hit a harbor town 35 miles from the Chinese border. No aircraft were lost over the town, Cam

Crewmen aboard the carrier *Kitty Hawk* move 1,000-pound Mk-83 and lighter bombs onto the flight deck for loading on aircraft bound for North Vietnam. In the right background are rocket pods, while the tail of a visiting A-3 "Whale" from VAH-4 stands out over the edge of the flight deck. Fuses will be inserted to the open nose cavities of these bombs after they are attached to aircraft pylons. (U.S. Navy, E.M. Weber)

Pha, but a Polish merchant ship in the harbor claimed to have been nearly struck by a bomb. Messages flew between Washington and the fleet regarding details of the incident.

Hitting so close to Communist China's borders was dangerous. Soon the Chinese began claiming numerous violations of their airspace by "United States imperialists." On April 12, a KA-3B tanker was declared overdue from a flight from the Philippines to the *Kitty Hawk*. Shortly afterwards, the Chinese claimed the destruction of the aircraft as it flew into Chinese territory. Protests were lodged by

In a carrier's flight operations room, scale templates of each aircraft on the flight and hangar decks are moved around to indicate the actual planes' positions on the ship. These men, in telephone contact with the flight and hangar deck, are responsible for "fitting" almost ninety aircraft aboard the carrier *Kitty Hawk* and getting the right plane to the right place at the right time. (U.S. Navy, W.J. Calligan)

the State Department, but the Communists maintained that the plane was attacking Chinese fishermen on the high seas in the Gulf of Tonkin.

Normally tankers were unarmed, but they still retained their weapons bay, and the United States never denied outright that the Skywarrior was armed. This was not the first time such a situation had occurred. From time to time, there were claims and counterclaims of shootdowns and harassment. (It is probably true, too, that American pilots in hot pursuit of escaping MiGs, may have inadvertently—or perhaps intentionally—chased their quarry into Red China.)

The A-6 Intruder was obviously an important new part of the carrier offensive, and acts of individual courage and fortitude were part of the mission. On April 27, 1966, a VA-85 A-6A took a hit from flak during an attack north of Vinh. The B/N, Lieutenant (j.g.) Brian E. Westin, looked over at his pilot, Lieutenant William R. Westerman, as the plane rocked back into an erratic climb. Westerman's oxygen mask was off, his face was white, and his left arm limp.

The B/N undid his harness and reached across to the control stick, guiding the A-6 towards the North Vietnamese coast while broadcasting for help over the radio. The semi-conscious Westerman roused himself sufficiently to set the power controls for the trip back to the *Kitty Hawk*. Escorted by its section leader, the crippled Intruder proceeded towards the waiting carrier.

Finally, with the squadron CO anxiously orbiting, the two men ejected. Once in the water, Westin noticed that Westerman was gradually weakening from loss of blood. The rescue helicopter hovering overhead created a downwash, making things a little more difficult for Westerman. Although Westin was already aboard the chopper, he jumped back into the water to help his pilot into the rescue sling. With Westerman safely aboard the Sea King, the B/N waved the aircraft away to get the pilot to medical attention as quickly as possible. A second helicopter appeared soon afterwards and pulled the tired Westin to safety—none too soon, for sharks, possibly drawn by blood in the water, had begun to appear. For his courage and fortitude in saving the life of his pilot, Westin was awarded the Navy's highest commendation, the Navy Cross.

During April, a major change in battle orders was instituted which, in effect, divided up North Vietnam target areas. The Navy was given the responsibility of keeping the coastal area, especially Haiphong, under attack, while the inland targets, Hanoi and the area west of the capital, were put under Air Force cognizance. This delegating of responsibility made a certain familiarity possible for pilots who flew over the same area regularly. Therefore, slight, but possibly important, changes in routine and equipment, could be noticed more readily. Another related bonus was a reduction of losses as the same crews flew the same routes, getting to know the various defenses and the best ways to avoid them.

5

Escalation to Escalation

The air-combat situation took another step when the first MiG-21s were sighted in March 1966. The delta-tailed fighters kept their distance, however, until April 26, when two 21s attacked three Air Force Phantoms escorting two RB-66s. One of the Phantom pilots fired two Sidewinder missiles at one of the MiGs; the pilot was soon seen to eject from his stricken plane. Several MiG-17s had been shot down prior to the April 26 clash, but this victory over the much more advanced 21 by the larger, supposedly less agile F-4 showed that in the hands of better trained pilots, the F-4 could hold its own.

The Navy, however, had not scored a kill since October of 1965, and the increased presence of MiGs brought hopes of rectifying the situation. The four MiGs credited to the Navy were shot down by three Phantoms and one A-1 Skyraider. The Navy's other major fighter aircraft, the Vought F-8 Crusader, although it had been in action since the very beginning of the fighting, had yet to score. On June 12, 1966, Commander Hal Marr, the CO of VF-211 aboard the *Hancock* gained the first F-8 MiG kill.

Flying escort for a force of A-4s, Marr and three other pilots of VF-211 saw four MiG-17s commencing low-level attack runs from below the 3,500-foot clouds which covered much of the route. Turning towards the oncoming MiGs, the F-8E pilot fired off a Sidewinder which missed, but a second missile blew the MiG apart from an altitude of only fifty feet. The Oregon native then turned his attentions to the other Communist fighters, and was firing his 20-mm cannons at a second MiG when his ammunition gave out. He was credited with a probable second kill.

The F-8 series was perhaps unique in that it was the last of its kind, the single-seat, pure air-superiority fighter, armed with guns developed for the Navy. It owed its birth to a 1952 Navy requirement for a supersonic interceptor and eventually the aircraft equipped thirty-six Navy and Marine Corps squadrons. The prototype flew for the first time in 1955, reaching Mach 1 on its initial flight. The number of Crusader squadrons grew, as did the number of variations of the basic airframe. A major design change was the reconnaissance model, originally called the F8U-1P, later changed to RF-8A. Equipped with several different aerial cameras, this variant formed a vital link in the chain of operations and will be discussed in succeeding pages. The fighter variants fought throughout the Vietnam War, gaining increased firepower, uprated engines, and additional radar capabilities along the way.

In the early years of Vietnam combat, however, the models of the Crusader serving with the Seventh Fleet carriers were, for the most part, Cs, Ds, and a few Es, equipped with four 20-mm cannon and two to four Sidewinder missiles loaded onto "Y" racks below the cockpit on the fuselage. This was to remain the Crusader's basic armament configuration throughout its career.

VAMPATELLA'S MiG KILL

Nine days later, on June 21 Commander Marr's wingman on the 12th, Lieutenant (j.g.) Philip V. Vampatella of Long Island, New York, shot down the next MiG-17, providing one of the most dramatic MiG encounters to that time. Vampatella was part of a flight of Crusaders called in to cover a rescue attempt of an RF-8 pilot shot down earlier. Orbiting the area in low clouds, and well within the envelope of North Vietnamese defenses, the four VF-211 fighters waited for the arrival of the rescue helicopter.

Suddenly Vampatella felt his plane shudder as he took a hit from flak, but he continued with his flight. Shortly thereafter, he and his section leader, being the lowest on fuel of the flight, prepared to detach themselves to find a tanker to refuel and return. However, the two F-8Es had barely set course for the tanker when they heard a "Tallyho, MiGs!" The remaining section had spotted MiG-17s approaching the area and was preparing to meet the Communist fighters. Vampatella and his section leader turned back to join their comrades, but Vampatella quickly found that his aircraft could not keep up with his leader, evidently sustaining more damage than he had originally suspected.

The other Crusaders and MiGs had already joined battle when he arrived, some 30 seconds behind his leader, and as he swung his plane around he spotted a MiG closing on an F-8. Not knowing who was in the threatened American plane, Vampatella broadcast a frantic call for all Crusaders to break right. However the call was not in time, and the Crusader went down.

Angry and frustrated, the young Navy pilot next saw another MiG-17 closing from the classic six o'clock position, directly astern. Wrapping his plane into a tight diving turn Vampatella headed for the ground, his stricken aircraft bucking and yawing. With his altitude right down to the trees and his airspeed 600 knots, he pulled out of his dive, and apparently had lost the MiG. As he settled down, and looked around, he saw his would-be attacker behind him and evidently headed for home.

Quickly deciding against the safer route of returning to the carrier and finding a tanker to replenish his fuel supply which was nearly gone, Vampatella went after the MiG. He closed rapidly on his prey, fired off a Sidewinder and watched the North Vietnamese plane disappear in a large cloud of smoke.

The elated pilot immediately set course for the coast, hoping he could locate a tanker before his

Sidewinder air-to-air missiles are checked out aboard an F-8E Crusader on the flight deck of the *Hancock*. This Crusader is from VF-211. It is sitting on one of the *Hancock's* catapults, ready to take off should shipboard or AEW aircraft radar indicate Communist aircraft coming out over the Gulf of Tonkin. (PH1 Donald Grantham, USN)

engine flamed out from lack of fuel. With about eight minutes of fuel remaining, he found a tanker and, after some initial difficulty, plugged in. However, the tanker could only give him enough to gain a few more minutes of flight. The *Hancock* was some sixty miles away and with damage to his horizontal stabilizer inhibiting controllability, Vampatella was not sure he would make it safely back to the carrier.

Happily, he arrived safely, and found that his tail had taken a direct hit from a 37-mm antiaircraft burst, with about eighty smaller holes from shrapnel dotting his Crusader's surfaces. The episode was recorded in countless newspaper articles. Perhaps the heroic aspect, the fact that Vampatella chose to go after the MiG instead of home, with critical fuel and damage problems facing him, gave the story

A MiG-17—allied code name Fresco—pursued by Navy F-8E Crusaders. In the air war over North Vietnam the American pilots, aircraft, and tactics were generally superior to those of North Vietnam. However, the latter's planes profited from strict U.S. rules of engagement and an extensive ground-based radar and intercept control network. (U.S. Navy)

something the American public could identify with. Whatever the reason, the young fighter pilot was a bonafide hero and was awarded with the second Navy Cross for air action in Vietnam. Bulletin boards around Pensacola, the training facility for all neophyte Navy and Marine flight crews, displayed glossy 8 × 10 photographs of now Lieutenant Philip Vampatella, gazing purposefully outward as he climbed into his trusty F-8, suitably autographed, "To the future MiG killers at Pensacola. Sincerely, Phil Vampatella."

MiG activity was definitely increasing, with the North Vietnamese showing more aggressiveness, obviously from gaining experience and some victories over American planes. However, the prime mission of the carriers was still attack. Ambitious operations were made against Communist supply lines, from trucks and rolling stock to bridges. With help from other units, such as E-2 Hawkeyes, the A-4 squadrons continuously harassed the Viet Cong truck convoys which ranged up and down the Ho Chi Minh trail. The hunt was particularly successful at night when the trucks would take advantage of the darkness to move in large numbers. VAs 153 and 155 from the *Coral Sea* were becoming specialists in this type of work. The Skyhawks would work in pairs, with one A-4 carrying flares which he would drop to light up the suspected target areas. With the trucks lit up for a few seconds, the second A-4 would zoom in and drop its ordnance. The method was quite successful and many trucks were caught and destroyed

Bridges were tempting and deceptive targets. Usually easy to spot on a run, and of obvious strategic importance, the various spans across the various rivers and waterways of North Vietnam, particularly those which carried rail traffic and link North Vietam with Communist China's supply lines, received a good deal of attention from the A-6 Intruders. The bridges were also heavily defended, and missions against them were among the most dangerous undertaken by any crews during the war.

On August 12, 1966, the Hai Duong bridge between Hanoi and Haiphong was dropped by one A-6 from VA-65. Flying at night, the crew put five 2,000-pound bombs on target and got away before the surprised North Vietnamese were able to fire a single shot. However, things did not always go so well or so safely, and the A-6s often found themselves devising violent maneuvers to escape the guns along the river banks. One crew, at least, came up with a drastic plan of action for countering any airborne threat. Trailed by a MiG bent on their destruction, they overflew an area of intense antiaircraft fire, hoping to discourage the MiG from following them into the briar patch. The method seemed to work, but of course the choice of using it was strictly up to the fortitude of the crew at the moment.

THE *POL* CAMPAIGN BEGINS

On Wednesday, June 29, 1966, Secretary of Defense Robert S. McNamara faced an expectant gathering of media reporters. He opened with the news

An SA-2 Guideline missile explodes near an F-4B from VF-151 based aboard the *Coral Sea*. Warning devices in the aircraft advised the pilot when there was SAM activity in the area and appropriate tactics could be initiated. (S. "Pete" Purvis)

that Navy and Air Force bombers had "inflicted heavy damage on three of North Vietnam's petroleum facilities." There had been one loss, an Air Force F-105, during the attack which covered Haiphong, Hanoi, and Dosan. With the attacks on Communist oil-storage complexes, the war had taken a new, meaningful, and obviously dangerous step. From the outset, U.S. military commanders had pressed for permission to strike at the very heart of the North's war machine, the oil and heavy-industry areas in the northeast.

However, President Johnson was reluctant to escalate the war by allowing strikes into the heavily populated areas. The North Vietnamese were more practical and in late 1965 and 1966 had begun building underground storage facilities as well as beefing up the construction of existing ones, in anticipation of increased American attacks. Photography provided increasing evidence that the Communists were bent on escalating supplies to their troops in the south; finally the President and Secretary of Defense gave approval, in April 1966, for the planning of petroleum and industry strikes. Permission to execute the attacks was withheld, however, mainly because the administration continued to be afraid of harming civilians within the targeted areas. It was only after two months of repeated discussions and assurances that the bombers could limit their bombs to within the specific areas, and that no third-country ships or personnel would be harmed, that Washington allowed the operation, known as Rolling Thunder 50, to commence.

Thus it was, that on June 29, 1966, aircraft from the carrier *Ranger*'s Air Wing 14 struck the Haiphong POL complex. With F-4s from VF-143 and VF-142 flying cover, the A-4Cs of VA-146 and VA-55 dropped nineteen tons of ordnance and five-inch Zuni rockets, all within eight minutes. One RA-5C reconnaissance pilot flying right behind the bombers later said, "It looked as if we had wiped out the entire world's supply of oil." Meanwhile, some seventy Air Force planes had taken off from bases in Thailand to strike at Hanoi's petroleum depot, North Vietnam's second largest such facility. By the time the *Ranger* had recovered her aircraft, word had been flashed to an anxious President that the entire strike force had returned safely.

In his news conference, McNamara had stated that the reason that permission was at last given to launch the attacks was "to counter a mounting reliance by North Vietnam on the use of trucks and powered junks to facilitate the infiltration of men and equipment from North Vietnam to South Vietnam." McNamara was evasive in answering questions about possible effects from other countries, whether there were any ships, besides the North Vietnamese ones, in the harbors, and whether other nations had been notified about the attacks.

The POL campaign continued throughout the rest of 1966 and on into 1967. The gloves had been taken off, finally, and the planes were being allowed to do what they had been designed to do. Large strikes in July and August took out major portions of the Communist facilities, as well as rolling stock, trucks, and river and canal barges being used to

The anti-bridge campaign: the Fan Wah bridge, essentially intact. Bridges made difficult targets, in part because of the heavy antiaircraft batteries sited near them. Numerous bomb craters are near the bridges. This photo — and millions of others like it — was taken by RF-8A Crusaders flying a couple of thousand feet high. (U.S. Navy)

transport men and supplies south. Photographs shown during press conferences and released to newspapers and magazines, showed huge columns of dense black smoke billowing up from the burning depots, some clouds as high as 35,000 feet.

All the carriers on station launched strikes with increasing regularity. The *Franklin D. Roosevelt* (CVA-42), *Constellation, Ranger, Hancock*, supplied Skyhawks, Intruders, and Phantoms to pound the Communists, from the DMZ to Haiphong. The pilots exulted at finally being turned loose.

But the sad, almost unfair, truth was that the strikes had come nearly a year too late. Deterred, perhaps, by an "over-coverage" of the matter by the press, the administration dragged its feet about committing itself to missions against the North's oil supply system. Within that time period, the Communists cached their precious fuel in various well-protected underground bunkers and tanks. That which was actually hit, was merely the tip of the iceberg. Hanoi had been able to disperse its stocks easily. Stepping up the number and size of the attacks only brought charges of harassment and murdering of innocent civilians from the propaganda-wise North Vietnamese. By year's end, General Westmoreland, in a frank addition to Admiral Sharp's report, could only say, "There is no lessening of enemy determination."

The newspapers were aware of the lack of progress in slowing down supply lines, and the mounting losses of men and aircraft which were making the air strikes very costly. McNamara himself was quoted as expecting to lose 580 aircraft by

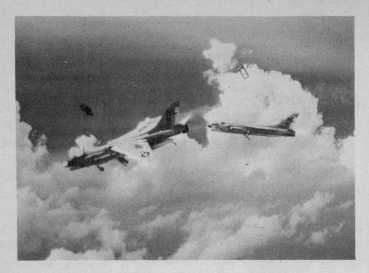

Sometimes the men came back when the planes didn't: Lieutenant Jack A. Terhune ejects from his crippled F-8E Crusader over the South China Sea in 1966. Just eighty seconds after parachuting into the water, he was picked up by a helicopter from the carrier and brought back aboard. An escorting F-8E fighter keeps position to observe the bailout. Note Terhune's cockpit canopy above the F-8E. (U.S. Navy)

year's end, at a cost (then) of over one billion dollars. Questioned by one senator, the Secretary declared that, yes, there was very little industry up north, but that the strikes were actually directed "principally against the lines of communication over which they are moving men and equipment into South Vietnam." The skepticism in the media was poorly hidden. One *Washington Post* column of September 20, 1966, asked "How Many Bridges Were There?" in regards to various bridges being attacked and reported as downed during the summer strikes. The same bridges were attacked but the North Vietnamese were adept at rebuilding the spans in a short time.

Although the papers admitted that the strikes had indeed destroyed much of the above ground POL areas, the columnists were quick to point that the missions were extremely costly. For instance: "It took 11 missions with a total of 40 airplanes last week to destroy a 50-car freight train near Hanoi." And the pilots were facing flak as thick, or thicker, than that encountered by crews over Germany in 1945.

A letter published by the magazine *Aviation Week & Space Technology*, and succeeding correspondence, written first by an Air Force F-4 pilot, then answered by a Navy Phantom pilot, threw out a lot of hard-hitting questions and facts. Why, the initial letter asked, was the Air Force risking two highly trained, very expersive pilots in one F-4? Why did these multi-million-dollar aircraft sortie with a minimal bomb load? "There is nothing more demoralizing than the sight of an F-4 taxiing out with nothing but a pair of 81s or 82s (250- and 500-pound bombs, respectively) nestled among its ejector racks." Sortie numbers seemed to be more important than results. The amount of aircraft a squadron or wing commander could point to as arriving over a target was evidently more important, than say, the number of barges and oil tanks destroyed. The Navy F-4 pilot whose letter was printed in a succeeding issue, confirmed the frustrated young Air Force flier's claims, while a young Marine second lieutenant completely rebuffed his fel-

Thousands of helicopters and fixed-wing aircraft were transported to Vietnam by ship, mostly aboard former escort aircraft carriers operated by the Navy's Military Sea Transportation Service. Here the aircraft ferry *Core* (T-AKV-41, formerly CVE-13) waits at anchor at Saigon to unload A-1 Skyraiders, T-28 trainers, and O-1E observation planes for American and South Vietnamese use. (U.S. Navy)

low pilots.

The letter writing, and the cynicism of the newspaper columnists, only contributed to the administration's previous reluctance to go after the enemy's resources in even greater efforts. And so, while the strikes did continue, they were not enough, and the Soviets and Red Chinese kept pouring supplies, guns, and aircraft across the borders or down the gangways of their ships. In September 1966, it was claimed that the USSR had doubled the size of North Vietnam's MiG-21 force, along with a contingent of 800 Soviet advisors and instructors.

An F-4J of VMFA-333 launches from a waist catapult during pre-crisis work-ups. The X.O. of VMFA-333 scored a kill during this cruise. (Dave Seder)

DENGLER'S ESCAPE

The summer of 1966 continued the attacks against the North Vietnamese industrial complexes and storage depots. Meanwhile, the Communists tried once more to carry out a PT-boat attack against American surface vessels on July 1. Phantoms from the *Constellation* sighted three P-6 boats as they began to run on the missile destroyer *Coontz*, 55 miles southeast of Haiphong. While the *Coontz* tracked the would-be attackers on radar, F-4s and A-4s strafed the PTs, sinking one boat and forcing the remaining two to retire, after launching torpedoes at the forlorn range of twelve miles.

Soon after the first boat sank, the aircraft found the other two and destroyed them as well. In an

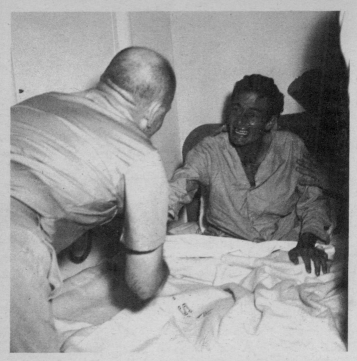

Lieutenant (j.g.) Dieter Dengler is welcomed back aboard the carrier *Ranger* after his escape from Laos. (U.S. Navy)

unusual twist in the war to this day, the first North Vietnamese prisoners of war were taken by the American ships. The number of American flight crews captured by the Communists was steadily increasing; increased strikes brought increased losses. There was very little hope of prisoners returning while the North was under such concentrated attack. And so it was with understandable pride and emotion that the country greeted the escape and subsequent return of Lieutenant (j.g.) Dieter Dengler in late July.

Dengler, a German-born American, had launched from the *Ranger* on February 1 in an A-1H Skyraider as part of an interdiction mission near the Laotian border. Ground fire severely damaged his plane, and Dengler was forced to crash land in Laos. After initially evading capture through the night, he was finally caught by Pathet Lao troops, who tortured the American pilot as they force-marched him through several villages. Arriving at a jungle camp, Dengler was thrown together with other men, some of whom had been held prisoner for more than two years. Throughout March, April, May, and June, the prisoners survived the continuous harassment, planning eventual escape should an opportunity present itself.

On June 29, after hearing of a plan to kill the prisoners, Dengler and his fellow captives made their escape in a hail of gunfire in which six of the Communist guards were killed. Wandering in the dense jungle, Dengler, severely ill with jaundice, picked his way towards what he hoped was freedom, living on fruits, berries and some rice he had managed to save during his captivity.

They floated down river on a raft they had constructed, eventually coming to an abandoned village where the men found some corn. After a night's rest, Dengler and an Air Force pilot, 1st Lieutenant Duane Martin, who was sick with malaria, made their way downstream to another village. This settlement was occupied, however, and the two Americans were suddenly attacked by a villager with a machete. Dengler managed to escape back into the jungle, but his comrade was fatally wounded by the assailant.

Alone, frightened, and on the edge of despair, Dengler made his way alone. It had been 18 days since his escape from the Pathet Lao prison. By the twenty-second day, his strength almost gone, Dengler was able to form an SOS with some rocks. He could go no farther and waited to be rescued or die. Luck finally was with the young pilot, for by late morning, an Air Force A-1E spotted the signal and directed a helicopter to pick up Dengler. He weighed ninety-eight pounds; when he left the *Ranger* five months before, he had weighed 157.

Dengler's rescue and story of survival and determination electrified the country. Eventually, he was returned to flying status. Much of what he had learned about survival was incorporated into the curriculum at various military survival camps. It was obvious that although a man who was shot down stood a good chance of being captured, it was also true that the will to survive was a strong, almost primitive, driving force from within, and if properly channelled, could sustain a downed flier through rough times.

Summer became fall, at least as the seasons were measured in the States, but on Yankee Station, the war continued. For the Navy, air-to-air combat was sporadic, after the initial flurries earlier in the year. In fact, there had been only one Navy MiG kill since Vampatella's score in June. (The Air Force, however, had its hands full during this time as MiGs were in the air constantly over Hanoi from September to December; six MiGs were downed during the period from July to September.)

On October 9, 1966, Commander Richard Bellinger, CO of VF-162, gained the Navy's first victory over a MiG-21. The kill was especially satisfying for the forty-two-year-old pilot because he had been forced to eject from his aircraft on July 17, when a MiG-17 got on his tail during a swirling dogfight and shot the F-8 full of holes. He was able to regain control of the damaged fighter, but after rendezvousing with a tanker, was unable to deploy his in-flight refueling probe because of damage. His fuel gone, Bellinger ejected forty miles from Da Nang.

Now, three months later, Bellinger was looking for revenge. Flying escort for a strike group from *Intrepid*, Bellinger and three other F-8s, acting on vectors from an E-1 Tracer, intercepted MiGs. Climbing to meet the North Vietnamese fighters, which were at 3,000 feet, Bellinger picked a single MiG-21 off to his right. The MiG, apparently spotting the onrushing F-8, broke off his attack on the strike force. As the 21 rolled inverted, split-essing towards the ground, Bellinger followed and fired two Sidewinders. Unable to follow the missiles, Bellinger righted his Crusader, as the Vought fighter screamed over the rice paddies and the wreckage of the MiG-21. Aboard the *Oriskany* once again, the elated CO said, "I've waited twenty years for something like this. It was a tremendous feeling." It was, indeed. Having flown B-17s and B-25s in World War II as an Army pilot, Dick Bellinger had traded his silver wings for Navy gold and had also flown

131

combat in Korea. In his third war, he had finally connected.

Two and a half weeks after Bellinger's victory over the MiG, *Oriskany* fell victim to a threat which

An F-8E Crusader of VF-162 is catapulted from the carrier *Oriskany* on Yankee Station in the Gulf of Tonkïn. Another Crusader is readied on the starboard "cat" while a third Crusader and an A-3 "Whale" wait their turns to launch. The *Oriskany* was the last of the twenty-four war-built *Essex*-class carriers, her construction was halted at the end of the war and she was not completed until 1950. This photo was taken in July 1966, shortly after her arriving on Yankee Station. (U.S. Navy, F.L. Blair)

stalks all carriers — fire. On October 26, a fire was touched off in a storage locker as two seamen returned some unused parachute flares from a recently recovered strike. (One Washington columnist later wrote that sources he talked to claimed that the two young sailors were "playing catch" with the flare when it ignited. In a moment of panic, one of the youngsters threw the burning flare into a locker.) The resultant fire spread into the nearby hangar bay, touching off other ordnance nearby. The flames burned through four levels, reaching the officer staterooms. Many of the pilots who had just returned from the mission were caught, unable to

escape the fire. Altogether, forty-four men died, including the Commander of Air Wing 16. (Dick Bellinger later assumed command of the wing.) The ship was saved from further loss of life by the quick action of the crew in combating the fire. Two helicopters were destroyed and four A-4s were damaged. *Oriskany* made her way to the Philippines for minor repairs, and then headed across the Pacific to the San Francisco Naval Shipyard for major rework.

MARINE AVIATION

Marine aviation continued its primary mission of supporting ground units. In late 1966, there were five A-4 squadrons operating from Chu Lai, VMA-121, 211, 214, 223, and 311. In fact, when the pilot of an A-4 set his aircraft down at 2:30 in the early morning of December 7, he had completed the field's 100,000th A-4 mission since its opening in June 1965. The Skyhawks were equipped with a radar control system which enabled ordnance delivery in bad weather or at night, thereby increasing the aircraft's effectiveness.

The UH-34D continued to be the main helicopter used for assaults and supply missions, although CH-46s carried their share of the load, especially when larger groups of men needed to be transported. On September 4, a CH-46 pilot earned the Distinguished Flying Cross when he rescued a squad of Marines trapped under heavy Communist fire. Making three pickups, he was able to retrieve all the Americans. The larger helos required support from fixed-wing aircraft, and the A-4s and larger F-4s obliged.

A case in point was the action in September, when a VMA-214 pilot earned a DFC for covering a CH-46 rescue of more than thirty soldiers. The A-4 pilot turned on his lights and strafed the Viet Cong positions in a successful effort to attract attention to himself, thus diverting the Communist ground fire from the trapped Sea Knights.

Besides the larger helicopters, the smaller UH-1 were utilized for a variety of missions, including fire support and an unusual program, nicknamed "Hol-

A formation of CH-46 Sea Knights from Marine Medium Helicopter Squadron (HMM) 165 fly off the Vietnamese coast during an operation in which they transported South Vietnamese Rangers into an area south of Danang. Designed to carry up to twenty-five troops or fifteen stretchers plus a crew of three, the CH-46s became operational in Vietnam in March of 1966. (U.S. Marine Corps)

lering Huey." These helicopters were equipped with loudspeakers which could be heard for a mile. Operating out of the Marble Mountain facility, two miles east of Da Nang, these UH-1Es flew over towns where Viet Cong were suspected of hiding, and with Vietnamese interpreters aboard, the small Bells flew over, warning residents of VC terrorism, as well as other items of interest.

The capability of Marine aviation in Vietnam was also greatly enhanced with the arrival of the first A-6s on November 1. Landing at the main Marine base in South Vietnam, Da Nang, VMA(AW)-242 and VMCJ-1 began operations two days later.

SEAWOLVES AND ACVs

Two unusual units which also made their debut in 1966 were the Seawolves and the SK-5 Air Cushion Vehicles (ACVs). The Seawolves, flying UH-1B Iroquois helicopters, were part of Operation Game Warden, which in turn was part of Market Time, the surveillance program aimed at reducing Viet Cong supply routes to the South. The Seawolves provided fire support and reconnaissance for river patrol craft and were especially effective against river traffic, such as sampans and junks, making their way down the Mekong River.

Originally trained by the Army, the Seawolves soon assumed control of their mission. In one action, three Hueys of HC-1 sank twenty-three sampans and destroyed twenty-five storage structures along the river.

Helicopters became invaluable in Vietnam for carrying troops and supplies rapidly to remote areas, faster and with less risk from ambush than with surface transport. Here a Marine CH-46 Sea Knight delivers supplies to a Marine ground unit atop a mountain in the northern section of South Vietnam. A second CH-46 is just visible above the one in the foreground. (U.S. Marine Corps, Joe Collins)

An additional Seawolf squadron was HAL-3, Helicopter Light Attack Squadron Three. Flying their Hueys from river vessels such as LST's, this squadron's crews made things difficult for the Viet Cong in the Mekong Delta. Usually operating in support of River Patrol Boats (PBRs), the various Dets, or Detachments, of HAL-3 were usually only minutes away from the action. Armed with .30-caliber machine guns in twin and single mounts, hand-held machine guns, and 2.75-inch rockets, the

A Navy Patrol Air Cushion Vehicle (PACV) speeds along the My Tho River in South Vietnam's Mekong Delta. The PACV could travel over water, swamps, and flat island land at speeds of almost 60 mph. Manned by a crew of five, the PACV was armed with several machine guns and grenade launchers. The propeller for propulsion is mounted aft of the gunner and just forward of the tail planes. (U.S. Navy, B.W. Wendell)

Seawolves operated in pairs for mutual protection.

Working in shifts the crews, two pilots and two gunners per plane, sometimes flew six to eight sorties a day — and night. HAL-3 maintained seven detachments, with a total aircraft complement of twenty-two Hueys on various LSTs in the Delta.

ACVs were totally new additions to the war, beginning operations in May 1966. Manufactured by Bell Aerosystems, these odd-looking machines, three of which were supplied, offered great speed, endurance, and the ability to traverse areas which normal waterborne vehicles could not go. With shark's teeth painted on their bows and armed with .50-caliber machine guns, the thirty-nine-foot-long craft operated in the Mekong Delta region, scouring the coastline with their high-resolution radar searching for enemy supply movement. Eventually, the Navy's Coastal Division 17, which operated the unusual ACVs in the Plain of Reeds south of Saigon, was moved north to Tam My, south of Da Nang, to stop Viet Cong infiltrators in that area. Described as "one-third airplane, one-third helicopter, and one-third boat," the ACVs were powered by General Electric LM-100 turbine engines similar to those used on helicopters.

A Navy PACV inspects a sampan in South Vietnamese waters for possible contraband. The Navy's three PACV's began operations in Vietnam in May 1966. Note that the flotation cushion is deflated and the forward door to the cockpit is in the raised position. (U.S. Navy)

Flying low: a Navy PACV and two UH-1B "Seawolf" helicopters head for the Special Forces base camp near Moc Hoa after searching for Viet Cong forces. (U.S. Navy)

An armed UH-1B "Huey" helicopter flies with the door gunner at the ready. This "navalized" helicopter is assigned to Light Helicopter Attack Squadron (HAL) 3, operating in the Mekong Delta. Note the machine guns and rocket tubes affixed to the side of the helicopter. (U.S. Navy, V. McColley)

Airman Robert Nunes loads an ammunition box for M-60 machine guns on a UH-1B "Huey" of HAL-3. In front of Nunes, a door gunner, are boxes of 40-mm M-79 grenades, fired from hand-held grenade launchers. Vietnam experience led to development of the helicopter gunship concept, personified by the Bell SeaCobra and Cobra, and the Mil' Mi-24 Hind series. (U.S. Navy, Dan Dodd)

The tank landing ship *Garrett County* (LST-786) and other ships and barges served as floating bases for the Navy's riverine forces in the Mekong Delta area. Here the *Garrett County* tends to the needs of UH-1B "Huey" helicopters and river patrol boats. Note derrick installed forward of the bridge on the starboard side to lift small craft onto the LST's deck. (U.S. Navy, T.S. Storck)

An A-1 Skyraider is lifted off the *Core* and lowered onto a waiting barge. The former jeep carrier transported seventy aircraft on this particular transit. The MSTS ships were civilian-manned by Civil Service crews. Note the preservative materials covering the Skyraiders to protect them from salt and spray during the Pacific crossing. (U.S. Navy)

6

Policy and the Continuing Air War

As the military clamored for greater action, the Johnson Administration seemed to be working counter to the general prosecution of the war. Admiral Sharp, in charge of the Pacific forces and an outspoken, increasingly critical senior officer, called for greater interdiction efforts. Citing the need to hinder external assistance to North Vietnam from China and Russia, to stop the flow of supplies south to the Viet Cong, and to destroy the North Vietnamese capacity to make war. Sharp noted the necessity of destroying six basic areas or "systems" in the North: electric power, war industries, transportation, military bases, oil storage, and air defense. All needed to be hit harder and more often.

The initial free zone around Hanoi, in which no bombs could be dropped, was another sore point. More military commanders agreed that, even with strikes on important industrial areas outside the

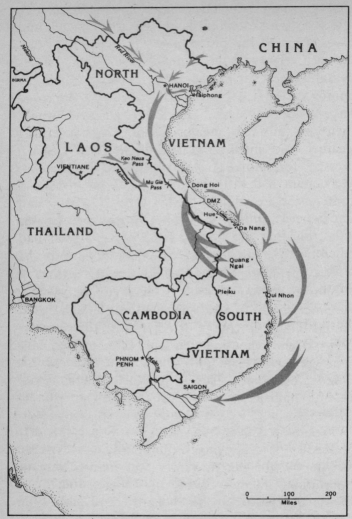

The Ho Chi Minh Trail

city, until major civilian centers of population were affected, the Communists would stick it out and never come to the peace table.

Sharp proposed in January 1967 that targets within his list of six so-called systems should be approved as packages, rather than being approved on a piecemeal basis. He claimed that he would then be allowed greater flexibility concerning weather and intelligence variations. While Sharp pressed for more strikes, Secretary of Defense McNamara had difficulty during Washington news conferences explaining higher aircraft losses and war policies. On February 15, when asked if he was indicating that the strikes of the previous year had failed, McNamara gave a lengthy dissertation on the prior objectives of the bombing program: raise South Vietnamese morale, reduce the flow of supplies to the south, and make the North understand the futility of any attempt to subjugate South Vietnam.

The next question dealt with what the reporter termed "rather confusing figures" on aircraft losses. In answer to this question, McNamara ran the historical gauntlet from World War II, Korea and onward, dividing aircraft into fixed wing, transport, reconnaissance, and various other types. Somewhere in all the explanations was an answer; McNamara was desperately trying to reassure a doubting Congress that aircraft production was well ahead of combat losses in Vietnam.

However, columnists, such as Carl Rowan in an article in the May 25 edition of the *Chicago Daily News*, questioned the economics of "raining millions of dollars worth of explosives" on the industrial areas, without seeing a definite effect. Indeed, Rowan said, ". . . the Pentagon estimates there are now 50,000 North Vietnamese soldiers in the South, as against 11,000 two years ago." Referring to a loss of 544 fixed-wing combat airplanes at that time, Rowan wondered whether the loss of 200 airmen and 1.1 billion dollars in planes was a fair exchange for what seemed to be very little reduction, if any, of the North's insurgent activities. Other reports told of increased air defense systems, truck convoys moving along the Ho Chi Minh Trail with near impunity. One columnist called McNamara "a man looking into a long tunnel with no patch of light at the end."

Beneath all the wartime bravado, both the civilian administration and the military commanders were painfully coming to the terrible realization that the North Vietnamese could probably fight indefinitely, taking strike after strike, accepting cuts in supply routes, industrial ruin, and whatever else the American attacks brought. But as long as population centers, port facilities, major airports and agricultural facilities remained largely untouched, there could be no hope of bringing the Communists around.

However, in spite of pleas by Admiral Sharp and other senior commanders, Washington continued to dole out targets. On May 23, a ten-mile circle was imposed on Hanoi; inside of this circle no bombs could be dropped, a direct rebuff to the contention that only with direct attacks on the civilian population could the war proceed to a conclusion. Restric-

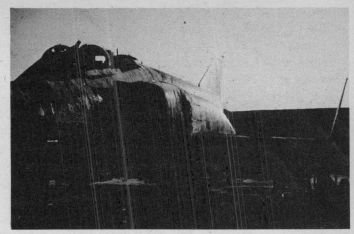

Naval air losses in Vietnam were not all in the air. Several hundred aircraft of all U.S. services were destroyed on the ground by Viet Cong guerrillas using rockets, mortar, and satchel charges. This F-4 Phantom from VMFA-115 was destroyed on the ground at Chu Lai in 1968.

An RF-4B of UMCJ-1 lands after a reconnaissance mission in 1967. Attached to MAG-11, the long-nosed RF-4Bs were operated only by the Marines; the Navy being afraid to fly the aircraft from carriers.

tions were also imposed on *when* certain targets could be struck.

The port of Cam Pha, an important North Vietnamese coal depot, could not be attacked when there were any foreign ships in the harbor. Naturally the North took advantage of this ruling and it was a rare day when a foreign ship was not tied up to a pier at Cam Pha. (Upon seeing the huge pile of coal in plain view at Cam Pha, one *Coral Sea* F-4 pilot recommended that defused napalm be dropped on the pile, followed shortly by several bombers. The bombers would drop their load and ignite the doused mountain of coal, and the result would be much like a huge barbecue fire started with lighter fluid. Although there was some official interest in this proposal initially, the plan never got beyond airwing level.)

Nevertheless, in June another incident at Cam Pha occurred when the Russians claimed that a merchant vessel had been attacked, resulting in the death of a crewman. Although an investigation was launched immediately, Washington could not prove that the ship had been attacked, even when Premier Alexei Kosygin presented President Johnson an expended 20-mm shell at a summit meeting.

The frustration of the men who risked their lives daily entering the intense corridors of flak and SAMs can be imagined, as they fought not only the enemy on the ground, but also the so-called rules of engagement laid down by their government. Even when ships in harbors opened up with 37-mm fire, the Navy pilots were strictly admonished not to fire back.

Downtown Haiphong was the target of precision strikes by naval aircraft. These photos were taken by RF-8 reconnaissance aircraft, showing minute detail of the vital port city. The main shipyard is immediately to the left of the explosions, on the lower side of the river. (U.S. Navy)

1967: MORE STRIKES AND AIR-TO-AIR COMBAT

As far as the Air Force was concerned, the new year of 1967 literally started off with a bang. In an elaborate operation (codenamed Bolo), several wings under the command of Colonel Robin Olds, a twenty-four-victory ace of World War II, shot down seven MiG-21s on January 2, depleting the North's inventory of that advanced fighter by nearly 50 percent. The action had been brought on by the heavy attacks on bomber strikes by MiGs which, after attacking, would run for the safety of their airfields which they knew to be off limits to the Americans. This situation was not unlike that in Korea fifteen years earlier when Communist fighters would retreat north across the Yalu River where U.S. pilots were forbidden to go.

Olds knew that the problem was to entice the North Vietnamese fighters into the air, where his Phantom pilots could shoot them down without restrictions. In what was called the first "pure fighter sweep" of the Vietnam War, Olds and his force, after duping the Communists into thinking the F-4s were really an F-105 strike group, met a large group of MiG-21s near Phuc Yen airfield, northwest of Hanoi.

Two more MiG kills on January 6 seemed to cause a temporary standdown in the Communist camp, and little MiG activity was noticed until March. However, by March the MiGs were up in force again, and it was clear that the airfields could no longer remain off limits. Thus, on April 24, aircraft from the *Kitty Hawk* struck the major MiG base at Kep, 37 miles northeast of Hanoi. Built by the Japanese in World War II, Kep had been a base for MiG-15s and 17s. The carrier planes struck the airfield, doing moderate damage to the 7,000-foot main runway and the support buildings. Two MiG-17s which tried to take off to intercept were shot down by VF-114 Phantoms. Aircraft from *Bon*

Throughout American participation in the Vietnam War, an offshore patrol was kept up by naval aircraft, seeking to identify all coastal shipping and, especially, ships entering and leaving North Vietnamese ports. Here a ship is looked over by a Navy P-3 Orion maritime reconnaissance aircraft. (U.S. Navy)

Homme Richard also hit Kep, damaging several MiGs on the ground, as well as downing two MiGs in the air.

The Air Force also struck Communist air bases, so that April and May became periods of ferocious air combat, as the MiGs rose to do battle with the strike groups. May 13 was a particularly successful day for the Air Force, as seven MiG-17s were downed by two Phantoms and five F-105s. The Air Force, in the six-month period of January to June, accounted for forty-six MiGs, a phenomenal number which caused Lieutenant General William

Momyer, Commander of the Seventh Air Force, to declare to a Senate committee that "we have driven the MiGs out of the sky for all practical purposes." The general's statement certainly seemed to be true. But the calm was short-lived. Resupplied by the Soviets and Chinese, and with new tactics, the North Vietnamese reappeared in strength in August, shooting down several U.S. aircraft during a strike against the Yen Vien railroad yards.

One of the problems the Air Force pilots faced was that many F-4s which would otherwise be used for air superiority had to be used as part of the bomber forces. The rule was that in the event of MiG sightings, the strike force was to increase speed to the target; if combat was unavoidable, the bombers were to still proceed to the target, and only when combat was joined, could the *last* flight jettison ordnance to attack the enemy. The bombers had to get through.

A Navy F-4 pilot at the time called the Air Force's tactics "inflexible." The bombers approached the targets in neat, close formations, and plodded through the flak, SAMs, and MiGs. This attitude of "pushing through" could also be found in aspects of electronic warfare. Whereas by 1967, the Navy had equipped each individual aircraft with electronic-countermeasure apparatus, the Air Force provided strike forces with a Spectre aircraft equipped with ECM devices. Thus, if the ECM bird was shot down or had to turn back, the safety of the entire flight was threatened. However, there was no denying the courage and skill of the Air Force pilots as they blasted MiGs from the skies. Even the heavy

This is the view from the right-hand seat of an A-6A Intruder making its final approach to land aboard the *Franklin D. Roosevelt*. Note the clear angled landing deck, permitting the plane to accelerate immediately and take off, should it miss all of the four arresting wires stretched across the deck. Numerous aircraft are parked forward and around the carrier's "island." (U.S. Navy, William R. Curtsinger)

F-105 Thunderchief accounted for its share of the Communists. During the same six-month period, F-105s shot down eighteen MiGs, most by 20-mm cannon fire, a fact which served to finally convince both Air Force and Navy commanders of the value of an integral gun, as opposed to the more fashionable all-missile armament found on the existing Phantoms. Eventually the F-4E reached the Air Force, with a 20-mm rapid-fire cannon; the Navy continued through the entire war with only missiles aboard its Phantoms.

The Navy had gotten its share of MiGs during this frantic period, all scored by aircraft from one air wing, CVW-21 aboard the *Bon Homme Richard*, except for the two initial kills on April 24 when Kep was hit for the first time. One of two MiG-17s brought down on May 1 fell to an A-4 pilot who had joined the landing pattern above the Communist airfield. Lieutenant Commander Ted Swartz in a VA-76 A-4C, was firing Zuni rockets at aircraft on the ground when his wingman told him there was a MiG on his tail. Taking advantage of his airplane's tremendous roll rate, Swartz pulled above and behind his pursuer and quickly fired off more Zunis. The air-to-ground rockets slammed into the MiG, sending it to the ground.

The Navy scored six MiG-17 kills in May, all by F-8 Crusaders with the exception of Swartz's A-4 victory. A combat on July 21, 1967 is representative of the encounters during this period. Four F-8Cs of VF-24 were flying cover for a strike group of twenty-five bombers. The escort flight's leader, Commander Red Isaacks, the executive officer of the squadron, sighted a flight of MiGs climbing to intercept the group. Calling the bandits out to his fighters, he peeled off after the MiGs. Gaining a position behind one MiG-17, he fired off one of his four Sidewinders, and missed. Pressing the button again, the pilot found the second missile would not fire. Now down to two missiles, the frustrated aviator stayed on the Communist fighter's tail and fired off the third Sidewinder. This time the missile tracked perfectly and flew up the enemy's tailpipe. The MiG exploded in front of the Crusader.

An A-4F Skyhawk is readied on a catapult aboard the carrier *Intrepid* in the Gulf of Tonkin. The flight-deck crewman at right is adjusting the A-4F on the catapult with a steering bar. The plane has a centerline drop tank and bombs on its wing pylons. Note the 20-mm cannon in the wing root and the refueling probe. (U.S. Navy, John G. Jacob)

Mesmerized by the fireball, the elated Isaacks was startled to find tracers hitting his aircraft. Hauling the Crusader around, he began a head-to-head run with another MiG. At the last moment, the MiG snapped away from the collision course, diving for the deck. Two other MiG-17s had fallen to VF-24's F-8s that day.

MiG KILLS AND TOP GUN

Navy fighters were to claim five more MiGs during 1967, bringing the total for that year to seventeen. The disparity between Air Force and Navy totals of kills is not easy to explain, but the Navy was sufficiently disturbed about it to direct a study of the situation by Captain Frank W. Ault, who had commanded the carrier *Coral Sea* during a seven-month deployment to Vietnam. The so-called Ault Report, published in 1968, recommended several improvements, among them: increased missile reliability (another study showed that during that period, some fifty air-to-air missiles had been fired in combat without downing one enemy aircraft), more training in air-combat techniques, and the establishment of a school whose primary function was to provide advanced level training in these techniques.

Initially called the U.S. Navy Postgraduate Course in Fighter Weapons Tactics and Doctrine, this school became known as Top Gun, and occupied a hangar on the master jet base at Miramar, California, northeast of San Diego. The first class convened in March 1969. Special emphasis was placed on what one pilot called "old-fashioned dog-fighting with new-fashioned weapons." Originally established under the auspices of VF-121, the Pacific Fleet's training squadron for F-4 crews, Top Gun evolved into a comprehensive five-week course, involving classroom training and realistic sessions in the air.

Flight crews attending Top Gun flew their own airplanes against the instructors, usually recently returned Vietnam veterans, who flew small, highly maneuverable F-5 and A-4 aircraft, painted in representative camouflage schemes of Communist air-force aircraft. The F-5s and A-4s provided a good approximation to the smaller Communist fighters, such as the MiG-17 and MiG-21, which were providing most of the aerial opposition in Vietnam. In part thanks to Top Gun, the Navy's kill score improved in air-to-air combat. In 1968, the ratio of Navy kills to planes lost was about two-to-one; by 1972, when the action heated up again, and several classes of Top Gun graduates had reached the fleet, the ratio had jumped to twelve-to-one.

CUTTING THE ARTERIES

The decision was made in early 1967 to begin mining selected rivers to inhibit use of the waterways for transporting supplies. The increased tempo of air attacks on road and railway networks had forced the Communists to use the various rivers which led to South Vietnam. This river traffic was kept under constant surveillance, the subject being designated Waterborne Logistic Craft, abbreviated WBLC, and whimsically pronounced "wiblicks" by the flight crews.

The first river-mining missions were flown by A-6As of VA-35 from the *Enterprise* on February 23, with mines being dropped in the Song Ca and South Giang Rivers. Other mines were planted during March and April, some at night; eventually five fields were planted. However, the important ports of Haiphong, Hon Gai, and Cam Pha remained off limits to such efforts. Observation of the minefields revealed that the North Vietnamese began minesweeping activities in April and that very little traffic left the mined rivers. But the intention of slowing the movement of supplies was never realized, as the North Vietnamese simply used increasing numbers of trucks along the trails.

In March, a new missile made its combat debut. Named Walleye, the new weapon was a TV-guided air-to-surface glide bomb which enabled the pilot to see his target through the missile's TV eye, affording greater aiming accuracy during the missile's flight. VA-212 aboard the *Bon Homme Richard* delivered the first Walleyes in an attack against military barracks at Sam Son on March 11. Other targets were bridges, as well as follow-up strikes against the Sam Son barracks.

BRIDGE CAMPAIGN

The story of attacks on bridges by U.S. aircraft is an interesting but confusing tale. Bridges over rivers

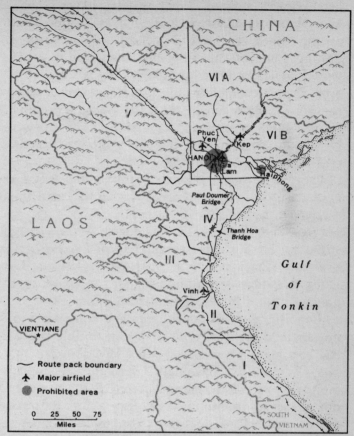

Route packs and major bridges in North Vietnam

161

and borders formed a major part of the North Vietnamese road system, and hence the supply route to the South. Initially, it seemed an easy task to destroy some of the more important spans, which would logically interrupt the supply effort. However, such was not the case. As happened in other aspects of the Vietnam War, the North's resourcefulness and ability to negotiate hardship were grossly underestimated by the American policymakers and commanders.

The Paul Doumer Bridge over the Red River at Hanoi carried a large share of rail traffic and thus received a great deal of attention from both Air Force and Navy aircraft. Damaged by an intense strike by Air Force F-105s on August 11, 1967, the bridge was back in operation by early October. The Doumer Bridge was attacked again, receiving more damage, but still remained largely intact.

Some bridges were destroyed, and some very important highway and railway links were interrupted. But the spans never stayed down very long, or new ones were built, seemingly overnight, to replace more seriously damaged structures. Some pilots reported seeing pontoons lined up along the river banks, waiting to be used to rebuild a damaged bridge. American newspaper writers could not understand why so many bridges seemed to be under attack. After all, there could not be that many bridges in the country. What the columnists could not see was the effort of the North Vietnamese who rebuilt bridges with surprising speed, thereby necessitating additional strikes.

One bridge, the Thanh Hoa Railroad Bridge over

the Ma River, 80 miles south of Hanoi, came to symbolize the heartbreaking frustration felt by U.S. pilots regarding the bridge campaign. In three and a half years from March 1965 to November 1968, when the bombing halt was instituted, nearly 700 sorties were flown against the Thanh Hoa Bridge at the cost of many aircraft. Although the bridge suffered damage from time to time, it resisted all efforts, some very elaborately planned, and remained standing and carrying traffic. The Navy tried its new Walleye missile on the Thanh Hoa Bridge in March 1967. Despite three direct hits, the bridge remained.

It was not until 1972, when attacks on the North intensified, that the fabled Thanh Hoa Bridge was finally destroyed. On May 13, Air Force F-4s attacked the bridge using so-called "smart" bombs, laser-guided weapons that homed onto laser beams directed at the target by a U.S. aircraft. But by this time, the Communists had built several backup networks around the bridge and so supply efforts were little affected by the destruction of the long-standing structure.

Frustrated in the attempt to gain permission to bomb Hanoi and Haiphong themselves, the military commanders came up with a proposal to "isolate" Haiphong, which still remained the most important area of supply concentration, by destroying the approaches outside the main area. Bridges, canals, and roads came under heavy attack, while the Communists responded with murderous antiaircraft fire, and rerouting supply convoys through Cambodia. Increased water traffic was also noted.

At this time of intense aerial attack, Haiphong evidently ran out of ammunition, for as the amazed flight crews struck the area one day, the usual curtain of flak and SAMs failed to greet them. The North Vietnamese had turned on the radar signals to fool the incoming force, but no missiles were fired and only minor 37-mm flak was encountered. For two days, the respite lasted. The weather precluded any strikes for the next three days. But when the rain cleared, and the strikes resumed, so did the flak. Haiphong had obviously been resupplied.

One result of the continuous attacks was the evacuation of nonessential civilians from Haiphong on August 25. Rumors began to circulate in diplomatic and media circles of an impending effort by the North Vietnamese to negotiate some sort of truce to relieve the pressure on its major port city. However, it was only a rumor, and the attacks continued, with sixteen Navy aircraft being shot down in August alone. On August 21, some eighty SAMs were fired at the bombing force. This tremendous concentration of missiles was in response to major strikes from *Constellation, Intrepid*, and *Oriskany* on Yankee Station. Everything from supply depots to railroad yards and airfields was hit, using bombs, rockets, and Walleyes. In August, PT-boat bases near Haiphong also came under attack by *Oriskany* A-4s, with three enemy vessels sunk.

Hanoi came in for its share of attention, and by late in the year, the capital had the distinction of being the most heavily defended city in the history of air warfare. With fifteen SAM sites constantly occupied, nearly 600 antiaircraft guns of all calibers, and various MiG-17 and MiG-21 airfields nearby, Hanoi presented a major test to every strike force sent to attack it. During this period, the weather, always a major factor, began to deteriorate and the A-6 was called in once more to become the prime attack aircraft.

Air losses continued during the intense strikes in mid-1967, and the specter of losses to Communist China reappeared in mid-August, when two A-6s apparently strayed over China's borders after a mission north of Hanoi. The Intruders were tracked by U.S. Air Force and Navy aircraft, and repeated warnings were broadcast, but the two American planes disappeared from the radar screens shortly after one of the pilots broadcast "Farmers, Farmers," the NATO code name for the MiG-19, over his radio. The Chinese evidently shot the A-6s down, and later reported that only one of the four crewmen had survived.

Half a world away in Washington, the war controversy swirled around the administration, and in particular, around Secretary of Defense McNamara. McNamara, one of the last remaining high-level officials of the Kennedy presidency, became what the *New York Times* called "a lightning rod for Presidential decisions." Indeed, McNamara took much of the stormy controversy surrounding the conduct of the war. Even at a Senate committee testimony in August, he staunchly defended the bombing policy. He explained the lack of proof that the North was affected seriously by the heavy strikes by pointing to the country's well-developed transportation system, ranging from bicycles to large truck convoys. As to road interdiction, McNamara said that "complete interdiction of these supplies has never been considered possible by our military leaders." Questioned about further escalation of bombing civilian centers, he replied, "Total bombing would violate America's limited aims in the war." The strikes against Haiphong, intended ostensibly to close the country's major seaport, would not totally succeed, he noted, as Haiphong was "a convenience rather than a necessity," indicating that much of the supplies imported through ports could be obtained over land routes.

Perhaps the most discouraging and telling comment made by McNamara was in regard to the effect the bombing campaign was having on the North Vietnamese, themselves. "As to breaking their will, I have seen no evidence in any of the many intelligence reports that would lead me to believe that a less selective bombing campaign would change the resolve of NVN's leaders or deprive them of the support of the . . . people. . . ."

Yet, the basic U.S. policies remained unchanged and the strikes continued. Taken by themselves, the attacks of 1967 accomplished a great deal; the Navy alone accounted for an estimated thirty SAM sites, 187 flak batteries, as well as 955 bridges destroyed (keeping in mind that many of the spans were dropped repeatedly as the North Vietnamese rebuilt them); locomotives, rolling stock, trucks, and watercraft destroyed numbered in the thousands. Fourteen MiGs had been destroyed in air-to-air combat. No less than eleven aircraft carriers had participated in the thousands of sorties over the

The AGM-62 Walleye glide bomb was the most accurate and effective air-to-surface weapon of its time, despite being unpowered. It was fitted with a self-homing television guidance system that controlled direction by moving control surfaces on the stub wings. The "missile," which carried an 850-pound warhead, is shown here during tests with an A-4 Skyhawk. (U.S. Navy)

North. The almost daily strikes had diverted civilians to air-defense duties in the North, civilians who would otherwise have been employed in activities in the South. Supply lines were affected, and the cost of operations in South Vietnam, still the main objective of the North, was increasingly more expensive. But somehow the Communists hung on.

THE SAR CAMPAIGN

While discussion and arguments continued in Washington, the strikes also continued in the South China Sea. And where and when the strikes occurred, there was an overwhelming need for Search and Rescue (SAR). As noted before, one of the major areas of success during the Vietnam War was the operation, constantly being refined, of an effective method of rescuing downed airmen who would otherwise be captured. The men who daily flew over highly defended areas, especially around what was called the "Iron Triangle"—Haiphong, Hanoi, and Thanh Hoa—needed to know that their chances of rescue, if shot down, were excellent.

An Air Force rescue team sets off over water for a mission in Vietnam. The HH-3E Jolly Green Giant is the USAF rescue variant of the Navy's Sea King while the escort consists of Air Force-piloted A-1 Skyraiders. The HH-3E is heavily armored, while the A-1s have rockets, as well as their 20-mm cannon, to provide covering fire. (U.S. Air Force)

A UH-2A Seasprite utility-rescue helicopter lands aboard the carrier *Forrestal* during operation in the Gulf of Tonkin. The helicopter, from Helicopter Combat Support Squadron (HC) 1, was based aboard the *Oriskany*. These "angels" stood by during flight operations to pick up pilots who came down at sea, but spent most of their time carrying mail and passengers. (U.S. Navy, Gary A. Phillips)

During the initial stages of the 1965 buildup, SAR efforts hinged largely on Air Force operations, using mainly HU-16 Albatross amphibians based at Da Nang. These twin-engined Grummans returned many downed pilots who ejected two or three miles offshore. Some were rescued in heavy seas and others under intense enemy fire from the shore.

However, as the war intensified and losses mounted, it was clear that an expanded SAR effort was necessary. By April 1965, a second SAR station was established; the first had been a roving SAR destroyer operating in company with A-1 Skyraiders. The older prop-driven aircraft were ideal for the long periods of flight necessary for SAR. The second station comprised Navy Kaman UH-2A/B Seasprite helicopters permanently stationed on a destroyer, able to reach a downed crewman in minutes. Additional improvements followed the first efforts. The first Sikorsky SH-3 Sea Kings began operations in November 1965, offering the ability to transport greater payloads, along with two-engine safety and longer range than the smaller Seasprites. Three larger helicopters operated from the carriers themselves, rather than cruisers and destroyers.

The little Seasprites were also modified to carry armor and machine guns to aid them under fire. Special teams of A-1s, A-4s, or later A-7s were established to fly near the strike routes to be on call to coordinate SAR missions. Then-Lieutenant Commander Rosario "Zip" Rausa, an A-1H pilot, recalled a particular day when he and his flight leader assisted a SAR attempt. Flying from the *Coral Sea* in 1967, the two Skyraiders had been on station for two hours, in company with an Air Force Albatross. Five minutes before another section of A-1s was to relieve them, the Navy pilots got a call to help a downed Air Force pilot forced to eject over North Vietnam. A Seasprite was to attempt the rescue, and taking their leave of the Albatross, the two Skyraiders headed toward Vinh and the helicopter.

At this point, the flight leader indicated he had lost his radio and passed the lead to his wingman,

The UH-2 Seasprite is picking up a sailor who was accidently blown over the side of the carrier *Constellation* by a jet blast. Some Seasprites were armed and armored for combat rescue missions into North Vietnam. But most in-country rescues were carried out by the larger and more capable Navy SH-3 Sea Kings and Air Force HH-3 Jolly Green Giants. (U.S. Navy, Ralph Wasmer)

An SH-3 with low-visibility markings and other modifications for the combat SAR role hovers over a submarine in the Western Pacific. Note the rescue hoist over the helicopter's open door. (U.S. Navy)

Rausa. The A-1s continued on and finally encountered the Seasprite which immediately called for them to follow him inland. Trying their best to keep the little green Kaman in sight, the two pilots weaved and bobbed, all the time looking for ground fire. After some time, the trio of Navy aircraft saw a rising column of white smoke from signal flares. Coming up on the area, the aviators saw an Air Force helicopter already on the scene, and as they stood by, the downed pilot rode the rescue hoist up into the other helo. Disappointed at not being able to make the rescue, Rausa remembered later, "The pilot was safe. That was the main thing." He also credited the crew of the Seasprite. "They did not hesitate. . . . they charged ahead in what I thought was a quintessential exhibition of courage." This action demonstrates that many aircraft from two different services converged to rescue a single pilot. The effort and success was the important thing.

In October 1966, a young pilot from VF-162 on the *Oriskany* had the dubious distinction of being rescued for the second time. Forced to eject from his F-8E on July 12, Lieutenant (j.g.) Robert Adams was picked up in the Gulf of Tonkin. Less than three months later, Adams was again forced to bail

An SH-3A Sea King helicopter from Helicopter Antisubmarine Squadron (HS) 84 refuels while hovering over the destroyer *Henderson* (DD-785). This technique enabled search and rescue helicopters to remain aloft over the Tonkin Gulf during carrier operations, especially when the helicopters could land on the larger cruisers to rest and refuel. The destroyer flight decks could not handle the Sea Kings. (U.S. Navy, E. P. Carr)

out of his Crusader when the plane was crippled by ground fire. (His first ejection was the result of a SAM hit.) Landing this time in a mountainous area, Adams hid from enemy troops.

With an umbrella of fixed-wing aircraft over his position, the young fighter pilot made contact with the rescue helicopter using the small personal survival radio each flight crewman carried. The foliage was so thick, however, that the chopper pilots were unable to see Adams and had to be directed by him to his position; it was not until he was in the rescue sling that he became visible to the rescue team.

Many SAR missions make exciting stories. On August 31, 1966 Lieutenant Commander Thomas Tucker, the Officer-in-Charge of the VFP-63 reconnaissance detachment on the *Oriskany*, was rescued from inside Haiphong Harbor itself. Tucker was flying a post-strike assessment photo mission when his RF-8 was hit by 37-mm fire, causing an immediate loss of control. Tucker barely managed to head the Crusader towards the open sea, but was finally forced to eject at only 1,500 feet. He landed only 150 yards from shore, in plain view of several junks and sampans. (The Communists offered a bounty of $200 for every airman caught by the fishermen.)

A Sea King from the ASW carrier *Kearsarge* was launched to rescue Tucker, who was soon under heavy artillery fire from the shore. Flying as low as 60 feet off the water, with shells arcing above him, the pilot of the helo spied Tucker's rescue flare and headed for him. At a height of only 30 feet, the big helicopter hovered long enough for Tucker to scramble into the rescue sling and be hoisted up into the aircraft.

Some SAR efforts, as intense as that which rescued Tucker were not so successful. On February 7, 1966, five A-4Es of VA-56 launched from the carrier *Ticonderoga* to attack targets in North Vietnam. Finding some railroad rolling stock, the Skyhawks dived on the targets. Flak batteries, hidden in the trees, opened up and hit one of the A-4s. The pilot, Lieutenant Ed Pfeiffer, tried desperately to make the Gulf of Tonkin, where chances of rescue were greater. But his controls froze and he was forced to eject. His comrades circled as he floated down, and were relieved to hear him on his survival radio. However, their relief was short-lived, as Pfeiffer told them he could see North Vietnamese coming for him.

A rescue helicopter had been notified and was en route, but time was too short. As one of the Skyhawks circled, directing the action, the others strafed the advancing Viet Cong. A pair of A-1s joined the frantic effort, and it looked as if the rescue might be successful. But the helicopter had not shown up, for the pilot was evidently lost. Out of ammunition, the Navy pilots made repeated mock strafing runs on the Communists. The downed pilot finally called that the ground troops were almost on him, and that there was nothing more to do. He was captured (and returned at the end of the war).

SAR efforts were largely successful. One of the most celebrated SAR missions occurred on June 19, 1968. Shortly after midnight, Lieutenant Clyde E. Lassen and his Seasprite crew from the destroyer

Preble got the call to go after a downed F-4B crew from *America* (CVA-66). The pilot and his RIO were hiding in dense foliage awaiting rescue. Lassen made his way in the dark, over unfamiliar terrain, with small-arms fire following him. The two downed fliers were about 150 feet apart, and as Lassen flew towards the first man, the flares which had been lighting the way burned out, plunging the struggling pilot into complete darkness. Fighting for control of the pitching Seasprite, Lassen got the helicopter on an even keel once more, as his crewmen fired machine guns into the night to repel the Viet Cong below.

Meanwhile, the two survivors had made their way to another pickup point in a more open area. Lassen brought the damaged helicopter down and waited under continuing fire, for the two men who were fighting their way across a rice paddy. The helo crew made some headway in silencing the enemy fire, and finally the two F-4 crewmen stumbled aboard the little UH-2. Lassen lifted off immediately and headed for his ship, finally landing with only five minutes worth of fuel remaining in the helo's fuel tanks. President Johnson presented Lassen with the Medal of Honor, the first such award made to a naval aviator in Vietnam.

Clyde Lassen was not the only naval aviator to receive the Medal of Honor for a rescue mission. The award was also presented to a Marine, then-Captain Stephen W. Pless, for action which occurred on August 19, 1967. Pless, a UH-1 pilot with VMO-6, answered a call to rescue Marines pinned down by Viet Cong on a nearby beach.

176

An F-4B Phantom, armed with air-to-air missiles and rocket pods, is towed across the flight deck of the carrier *Ranger* in preparation for launching. Three other Phantoms fly over the carrier, making their upwind approach for recovery after a mission over North Vietnam. (U.S. Navy, Donald F. Grantham)

Pless found forty to fifty Communists shooting at four Marines; he quickly began making strafing runs with rockets and machine guns, at levels so low that debris from the explosions hit his own aircraft. Finally landing to attempt a pickup, Pless waited until the men had gotten aboard, but his overloaded Huey settled back four times before he was able to take off. Pless was awarded the Medal of Honor on January 16, 1969, along with Lieutenant Lassen, and was promoted to major, becoming the youngest major in the Marine Corps at age 27.

SAR efforts were a major morale factor, as well as of sound military and economical value. The investment in training flight crewmen was considerable, and the possibility of having valuable intelligence forced out of these men during interrogation after capture made the effort all the more important. These SAR missions continued throughout the war. On June 7, 1972, a Sea King of HC-7 was prepositioned off the North Vietnamese coast. When configured for rescue operations, these large helicopters carried armor plating, a General Electric Gatling gun capable of firing 4,000 rounds per minute, and several M-60 hand-held machine guns. An RA-5C Vigilante reconnaissance aircraft had taken a hit from a SAM and the crew was heading the plane out towards the water before ejecting. The Sea King was directed to the expected ejection point and soon had in sight the crew of the Vigilante. Joined by a second chopper, which dropped a swimmer in the water to aid the navigator, the first helo scooped up the pilot. Although the swimmer had sustained injuries from jumping too great a height, he found the navigator, who promptly asked him, "How the hell did you get here so fast?" The Sea Kings were then beginning to draw fire from the shore, and a patrol boat was headed in their direction. Had the rescue been any later, it would have been *too* late.

Although mainly involved in surface activities for the Market Time Operation, the Coast Guard contributed a small group of its pilots and crewmen to the SAR effort. Assigned to the Air Force's 37th Aerospace Rescue and Recovery Squadron, the Coast Guard aviators flew HH-3E helicopters in several rescue operations. One pilot was posthumously awarded the Silver Star and the Distinguished Flying Cross for his efforts during his exchange duty with the Air Force. Lieutenant Jack Rittichier was killed during one of the squadron's rescue missions in 1968.

There are countless stories of SAR missions during the war, some routine, some not. But the SAR program was one of the few bright spots of the Vietnam War. After undergoing rigorous training, the SAR crews fought the boredom of waiting for a call, and displayed uncommon bravery and dedication in answering that call. Decorations were plentiful for many of the helo crewmen who risked their lives for others, but as one Navy writer put it, "There are undoubtedly any number of rescued pilots who feel that's not reward enough."

THE *FORRESTAL* FIRE

With the war in Southeast Asia providing experience for all phases of naval operations, several carriers which normally belonged to the Atlantic Fleet were occasionally routed to WESTPAC duty, and thus it was that on June 6, 1967, *Forrestal* left

The carrier *Forrestal* in the Gulf of Tonkin. Completed in 1955, the *Forrestal* was the first of the Navy's supercarriers. This photograph is believed to have been taken early on the morning of July 29, 1967. (U.S. Navy)

Tragedy strikes the carrier *Forrestal* shortly after her arrival in the Gulf of Tonkin on the carrier's first Pacific deployment. Flames and smoke spew from the carrier's after flight deck as the destroyer *Rupertus* (DD-851) comes alongside to assist. This tragedy cost the Navy 134 officers and enlisted men. (U.S. Navy)

Norfolk, Virginia, for what was to be her first combat deployment. Carrying Air Wing 17, *Forrestal* was the first U.S. carrier to be built from the keel up with an angled deck. She carried East Coast squadrons, two F-4B squadrons, VFs 11 and 74; VAs 106 and 46, flying A-4Es; RVAH-11, with RA-5C Vigilantes, for which the big carrier had undergone major modification for the IOIC reconnaissance intelligence system; the KA-3Bs of VAH-10; and VAW-123, flying E-2As. *Forrestal* arrived on Yankee Station on July 25 and immediately began combat operations, her aircraft flying 150 sorties during the next four days, without the loss of a single aircraft.

Just before 11 A.M. on July 29, the second launch was being readied when a Zuni rocket was accidently fired from an F-4 on the aft end of the flight deck, hitting an A-4's fuel tank. The tank erupted, spreading flames over half the flight deck. The fires caused ordnance to explode, and the flames, spread by the wind over the deck, engulfed the aft end of the stricken ship. Berthing spaces immediately below the flight deck became death traps for fifty men, while other crewmen were blown overboard by the explosion.

Nearby ships hastened to the *Forrestal*'s aid. The *Oriskany*, herself a victim of a tragic fire in October 1966, stood by to offer fire-fighting and medical aid to the larger carrier. Nearby escort vessels sprayed water on the burning *Forrestal* and within an hour the fire on the flight deck was under control. But secondary fires below deck took another twelve hours to contain. The damage and loss of life was catastrophic.

The four-and-a-half-acre flight deck was littered with pieces of aircraft, as men struggled to clear away bombs and ammunition, throwing the ordnance over the side. One chief petty officer spotted a bomb already being quickly surrounded by flames, and with only a small fire extinguisher, the man started towards the danger. The bomb exploded in front of him, killing him and several firefighters nearby. Ordnance was literally pulled off aircraft and thrown over the side. One young 130-pound lieutenant found the strength to heave a 250-pound bomb overboard.

Once the fire was under control, the time had come to tally up the loss of life and damages. One hundred and thirty-four men had lost their lives, twenty-one aircraft were destroyed and forty-three others damaged. The cost to repair the carrier was reckoned at $72 million. The *Forrestal* made her way to the Philippines and then home, arriving at Norfolk on September 14.

A special group, the Aircraft Carrier Safety Review Panel, was convened on August 15 to examine the problem of shipboard fires. The panel's findings were released on October 18, and among the recommendations made were: development of a remote-control fire-fighting system for the flight deck, development of more stable ordnance, improvement in survival equipment, and increased training in fire survival.

With the *Forrestal* heavily damaged and out of action, the remaining carriers *Constellation, Oriskany, Intrepid* and *Coral Sea*, the last of which had arrived on Yankee Station in September, continued the fight. Their aircraft flew against bridges, depots, SAM sites, and airfields, in an effort to inflict as much damage as possible before the monsoon set in again. Already by November the rains and low ceilings were back. Also in the back of everyone's minds was the approaching Christmas truce, a time when the Viet Cong would take advantage of the standdowns and boldly move supplies south in broad daylight. Intensive mining efforts were undertaken to deter supply traffic as much as possible before the truce period.

MORE NEW PLANES

The carrier *Ranger* arrived on Yankee Station on December 3, 1967, bringing a new aircraft to the air war—the Vought A-7A Corsair II. Although intended to replace the A-4 as the primary light strike aircraft, the A-7 in reality formed a partnership for the remainder of the war with the Skyhawk. The A-7A, although bearing a superficial resemblance to the F-8, was a totally new design which, like the F-4, was to be placed in production for the Air Force as the A-7D. As a matter of fact, as the *Ranger* arrived in the South China Sea, she included in the complement of VA-147, the first operational Corsair squadron, twenty-four Air Force personnel (including three pilots) to evaluate the aircraft for their service.

The *Ranger* A-7s flew strikes against coastal defense sites, truck convoys and in support of Marine

An A-7A Corsair lands aboard the carrier *Ranger* in the Gulf of Tonkin after a mission over North Vietnam. The VA-147 aircraft still has four rocket pods on its wing pylons, plus Sidewinder air-to-air missiles on its "cheek" attachment points. Note the superficial resemblance to the F-8 Crusader. The A-7's cockpit is closer to the nose and the wing does not move upward as in the fighter. (U.S. Navy)

ground operations soon after arrival, in concert with A-4s of other carriers. But time and the weather were against much of the effort, and only the A-6s flew on a regular basis. The worsening weather allowed the North Vietnamese to repair many bridges which had been damaged by the strikes; this naturally meant additional strikes by Navy aircraft.

MiG activity was constant, although not at the peak level of the summer months. Only three MiGs

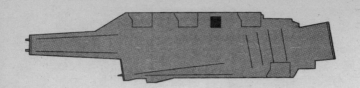

ENTERPRISE

The *Enterprise* (CVAN-65) was the first nuclear-propelled air-craft carrier, completed in 1961 to a modified *Forrestal* design. The ship had a distinctive island structure, without funnel and mounting the billboard-like AN/SPS-32 and AN/SPS-33 fixed-array radars (subsequently removed). No additional nuclear carriers were built until the *Nimitz* (CVAN-68), laid down in 1968 and completed in 1975.

Displacement: 74,700 tons light, 86,000 tons full load; length overall: 1,123 feet; propulsion: steam turbines, ~ 280,000 shaft horsepower, 4 shafts; reactors: 8 pressurized-water type; speed: 30+ knots; catapults: 4; elevators: 4; aircraft: 90

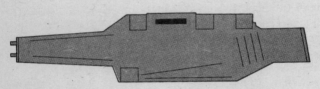

FORRESTAL Class

Eight ships of the basic *Forrestal* (CVA-59) design were completed from 1955 to 1968. Details and elevator arrangements differ, with the *Saratoga* (CVA-60) and later ships having high-pressure steam plants (1,200-pounds per square inch vice 600 in the *Forrestal* and previous carriers). The following characteristics are for the similar *Kitty Hawk* (CVA-63) and *Constellation* (CVA-64).

Displacement: 74,700 tons light, 86,000 tons full load; length overall: 1,123 feet; propulsion: steam turbines, 280,000 shaft horsepower, 4 shafts; boilers: 8; speed: 34 knots; catapults: 4; elevators: 4; aircraft: 80+

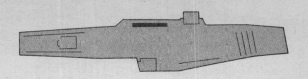

MIDWAY Class

Three war-built *Midway* (CVA-41)-class carriers were completed from 1945 to 1947. These ships were extensively modernized during the 1950s, receiving steam catapults, angled flight decks, strengthened elevators, etc. Details varied considerably after various modernizations and modifications. The following are *Midway* characteristics:

Displacement: 49,000 tons light, 62,600 tons full load; length overall: 979 feet; propulsion: steam turbines; 212,000 shaft horsepower, 4 shafts; boilers: 12; speed: 33 knots; catapults: 2; elevators: 3; aircraft: 75

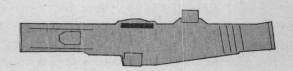

HANCOCK Class

Twenty-three *Essex* (CV-9)-class carriers were completed from 1942 to 1946 plus the *Oriskany* (CVA-34), completed in 1950. All underwent various degrees of subsequent modernization, with seven being upgraded to the 27C configuration during the early 1950s (angled flight deck, steam catapults, heavier arresting gear and elevators, increased fuel capacity, etc.). Of these ships seven were generally classified as the *Hancock* (CVA-19) class; their nominal characteristics were:

Displacement: 33,100 tons light, 42,600 tons full load; length overall: 899 feet; propulsion: steam turbines, 150,000 shaft horsepower, 4 shafts; boilers: 8; speed: 33 knots; catapults: 2; elevators: 3; aircraft: 70+

were downed by Navy fighters in the last three months of 1967. However, a Marine was able to chalk up that service's first MiG kill, albeit in an Air Force plane. Flying an exchange tour with the Air Force, Marine Captain Doyle D. Baker shot down a MiG-17 on December 17, while flying an F-4D Phantom with the 13th Tactical Fighter Squadron stationed at Udorn, Thailand. Baker, on his thirtieth mission over North Vietnam, was flying escort for F-105s when he spotted a low-flying MiG-17 and went after it. Using his 20-mm gun pod, he chased the Communist fighter, eventually using all his ammunition. Switching to missiles, he hauled his heavy airplane around in an effort to keep the twisting MiG in sight long enough to fire off a missile. After making an 11-g turn, he righted his aircraft and shot a Falcon missile up the enemy fighter's tail. (Baker's kill was the only Marine score until 1972, when another Marine exchange pilot, flying an Air Force Phantom, shot down a MiG-21.) The Marines' mission in Vietnam did not allow their pilots to engage enemy aircraft often, if at all. Flying in support of the ground units, Marine aviation and its accomplishments became lost in the day-to-day action and hot fire-fights on the ground. However, without air support, the Marine ground forces would have been hard-pressed indeed.

The Marines gained a new helicopter early in 1967 when four giant CH-53A Sea Stallions arrived at the Marble Fountain Facility in January. These four new aircraft of HMH-463 represented a quantum leap in the Corps' transport capability. By the end of the year, CH-53s had retrieved 120 damaged

UH-34s and CH-46s from combat areas.

Helicopters made the difference between life and death in some actions. Just after midnight on May 10, seven men of a reconnaissance team near Quang Tri, South Vietnam, had to call for helicopter evacuation after being attacked by Viet Cong. Three CH-46s were sent to rescue the Marines, and before the action was over the three aircraft had been hit, with one co-pilot killed, six crewmen wounded, and four Marines on the ground dead.

The CH-46, the first of which had arrived in March 1966 with HMM-164, came under some criticism due to a series of eight different accidents in mid-1967. The problem seemed to be with the helo's tail assembly which was subsequently strengthened along with other modifications. The workhorse UH-34, which had borne the brunt of initial operations, did not leave Vietnam until August 1969.

The Marine Corps, in an interesting sidelight, was making use of what was probably the second oldest tactical aircraft in Vietnam. Junior only to the EF-10B Skyknight, the Grumman TF-9J Cougar dated back to the Korean War, having been developed from the F9F-2/5 series of Panther jets. Arriving in the fleet just after the Korean War ended, the swept-wing fighters served in a variety of roles from fighter, to ground attack, to photo reconnaissance. However, by the early 1960s the Cougar was on its way to retirement, except for serving with some Reserve squadrons. A two-seater had been developed and was brought into service in the training squadrons where it served until 1969, alongside the

A trio of A-7B Corsairs from the carrier *Oriskany* release bombs over a target in North Vietnam. The paint scheme on the tails indicate different squadrons: the plane nearest camera is from VA-155 and the two others are from VA-153. (Tom Nelson)

more modern TA-4J Skyhawk.

In Vietnam, the Cougar continued to serve with the Marines, operating from Da Nang and then Chu Lai as a jack-of-all-trades, although its primary duties were those of Tactical Air Coordinator (TAC) and helicopter escort. Armed with cannon and rockets, the old jets also operated in direct support of the Marines on the ground, flying strikes against Viet Cong positions ahead of the American

An A-7A Corsair from VA-147 — the Navy's first A-7 squadron to deploy — streaks over the carrier *Ranger* steaming off the coast of Vietnam. The name Corsair has been used for Vought-built aircraft since 1926, with the F4U Corsair having been one of the best fighter aircraft of World War II. The French Navy flew that Corsair over Indochina in the early 1950s. (U.S. Navy)

The Hot Seat. The cockpit of an F-8 Crusader is small, cramped, and complex. This aircraft was flown by Commander Dave Perault, commanding officer of VF-24 aboard the *Hancock*. The two rings above the seat are handles to activate the ejection seat; the white rectangle forward of the seat is the radar screen. (Eliot Tozer)

Ordnance specialists service an F-8 Crusader from VF-24 aboard the carrier *Hancock* in the Tonkin Gulf. Beyond the F-8 is an unarmed RF-8 Photo Crusader from VFP-63. (Eliot Tozer)

forces. Used by Marine Air Group 11, the TF-9Js were sometimes painted with tiger-shark teeth on the nose.

By late 1967, however, the first TA-4Fs began to replace the aging Grummans, and the two-seater Skyhawks took over in fine style. There were instances of TA-4Fs circling near targets, directing shellfire from offshore ships of TF 77, and in particular the battleship *New Jersey* in October 1968. The World War II battleship had been brought out of mothballs to support shore operations. With her nine 16-inch guns she could obliterate any shoreline target. TA-4s also flew many visual reconnaissance missions over South Vietnam, searching for SAM sites and depots.

TA-4F of MAG-11 at Da Nang in 1968. The radio call-sign was 'Playboy,' hence the 'Rabbit' insignia on the tail. The TA-4F replaced the TF-9J in the armed reconnaissance role. (Dave Seder)

The CH-53 Sea Stallion, which arrived in Vietnam in early 1967, was the largest helicopter in U.S. military service until the three-engine CH-53E variant began delivery in the early 1980s. The helicopter can carry a maximum of some fifty-five troops or twenty-four stretchers. The Sea Stallions shown here are loading troops aboard the helicopter assault ship *Guadalcanal* (LPH-7). (U.S. Navy, Joe Mancias, Jr.)

A propeller-driven counterpart of the TF-9 and TA-4 was the Cessna O-1E Bird Dog, a high-wing, conventionally-geared aircraft originally used for peaceful liaison duties. The Air Force and South Vietnamese military used the Bird Dog for roughly the same missions. However, the Marines' original supply of O-1s reached the end of their service lines in September 1965, and the Corps had to hunt up additional aircraft, eventually finding a dozen. Overhauled and certified fit again for service, the O-1s were airlifted to Vietnam and served through

A CH-53A Sea Stallion of Marine Heavy Helicopter Squadron (HMH) 463 lifts a 155-mm howitzer weighing over six tons from the Marine base at Chu Lai to an advanced fire support base. The U.S. Army, Navy, Air Force, and Marine Corps employed several thousand helicopters in the Vietnam War. Note the streamlined lines of the CH-53A when its wheels are retracted and rear loading ramp is closed. (U.S. Marine Corps, Robert Leak)

some heavy fighting, including the siege of Khe Sanh in 1968.

The Marines also made use of World War II-vintage transports such as the C-47/117 Skytrain, the military version of the famed DC-3 airliner, and the C-54 Skymaster, the military DC-6. These old aircraft ran the daily, routine supply flights up and down the coast of South Vietnam, bringing food and ammunition to the troops in the field, as well as providing transport service for personnel on the move. It was a boring job, although sometimes the lumbering aircraft flew into Viet Cong ground fire while returning to their destination. The flight crews' outlook was very much enlivened by these occasional brushes with the enemy.

The Marines even included their own air-to-air tanker aircraft in the form of KC-130 Hercules, four-engine turboprop transports fitted with the Navy's basket-and-hose refueling apparatus. Marine Refueler-Transport Squadron (VMGR) 152 performed yeoman service refueling A-4s from Chu Lai which would lift off with maximum bomb load and reduced fuel, and then fill up from the waiting Hercules before continuing to their targets.

By the end of 1967, eleven carriers had participated in operations in Vietnam, with correspondingly high numbers of sorties, ordnance tonnage, and hours expended. However, though all the impressive figures told a heroic story, the hard fact remained that the Viet Cong had no desire to talk peace. Indeed, as the Christmas truce approached, it was obvious that the enemy was going to use the standdown, as he always did, to move men and

A pair of Marine A-4 Skyhawks are refueled in flight some 10,000 feet above South Vietnam by a KC-130 Hercules. Marine "Herks" from Refueller/Transport Squadron (VMGR) 152 provided air-to-air fueling of tactical aircraft as well as cargo and troop transport services in Vietnam. Refueling permitted the Skyhawks to take off with large bomb loads and minimum fuel. (U.S. Marine Corps, Carl E. Erickson)

supplies south without fear of hindrance from air strikes. Thousands of vehicles clogged the trails and waterways leading into South Vietnam, waiting for the truce period to begin. VFP-63 reconnaissance pilots and ground crews worked feverishly over the Christmas holiday, flying many sorties over the supply trails, each mission bringing back ample evidence of Communist activity. It was clear that the North Vietnamese were planning something big.

7

The North Vietnamese Attack

The reconnaissance flights over Christmas and New Year's confirmed what all the personnel aboard the ships of Task Force 77 knew: the Communists were pouring tons of supplies into South Vietnam. Trucks, sampans, and barges clogged every identifiable road, trail, river, and stream. Hardly had the New Year's truce period ended when strikes were launched, hopefully to repel the invasion of men and material. F-8s from the *Oriskany* used Sidewinder missiles, normally carried for air combat, against Communist rail traffic. The Sidewinder, a heat-seeking missile which homed on heat from exhaust emissions, was discovered to be very effective against locomotives, and the VF-162 Crusader pilots were credited with several engines destroyed. Activity was especially heavy during the period January 2–11, 1968, as aircraft from *Oriskany, Coral Sea,* and *Ranger* struck the bridges

"Huey" became synonymous with mobility, transport, assault, dustoff, and medical evacuation in the Army and Marine lexicons during the Vietnam War. Thousands of the Bell-produced machines served in the conflict. The name Iroquois was officially assigned, but the helicopter was always called "Huey," the name derived from the pre-1962 designation letters HU. (Bell)

around Hanoi and Haiphong, SAM sites, and storage depots.

While aircraft of TF 77 flew daily strikes against the Viet Cong, an event occurred in the Sea of Japan much farther north that momentarily diverted American attention from Vietnam. On January 22, the intelligence collection ship *Pueblo* was surrounded by North Korean patrol boats, and after a short exchange of fire, was boarded and taken to Wonsan Harbor. She was the first United States ship of war to be boarded and surrendered since the War of 1812. In response, six Naval Air Reserve squadrons were mobilized, and nuclear Task Force 71 was created, with the carrier *Enterprise*, steaming towards her third combat cruise off Vietnam, as its flagship. It appeared that the nuclear carrier might launch its aircraft in a retaliatory strike against North Korean targets, but that idea was abandoned when the *Pueblo* arrived in Wonsan Harbor. TF 71 remained in the Sea of Japan awaiting orders. The crisis soon evolved into a waiting game, with the North Koreans holding the American crew as hostages against air strikes.

Relieved by *Kitty Hawk* on February 6, *Enterprise* continued on her way, arriving on Yankee Station on February 21. By the time of her arrival, major battles in South Vietnam had already begun, heralding the long-awaited Communist invasion of the South.

TET AND KHE SANH

The Viet Cong finally struck on January 30, 1968 at various points in South Vietnam—Nha Trang, Pleiku, Da Nang, and Qui Nhon. The attacks were begun a day before the Vietnamese holiday of Tet, the lunar new year, on January 31. The Communists, in an elaborately planned ruse, had indicated a willingness to talk peace, and had kept the Americans off-balance during this period while they moved supplies and men south. Viet Cong even penetrated the American Embassy in Saigon on the

31st, but after initially blasting holes in the protective walls, were repulsed by American and South Vietnamese guards. All of the attackers were killed.

While mainly a land battle, with little or no naval or air activity, the 1968 Tet Offensive was part of an overall Communist attack. Although the Viet Cong pressed the assault, within two weeks, Communists losses were 32,000 dead and 5,800 captured. No sizeable territory had been gained by the Communists, and even more importantly, they had failed to rally the South Vietnamese populace to their side.

However, farther to the northwest, about six miles from the Laotian border, the embattled camp at Khe Sanh was literally fighting for its life as thousands of North Vietnamese attacked. Occupied by American forces since 1962, Khe Sanh was an important block to Communist supplies coming south from Laos, and although the Viet Cong initially tolerated the camp, with occasional shelling and sapper attacks, by 1967 it had become obvious that the camp had to be taken. Augmentation of American troops at Khe Sanh by the arrival of Marines in January 1967 only served to solidify Communist plans for a takeover.

When the first Viet Cong attacks began on January 21, 1968, a huge airlift operation was begun, by which it was hoped to supply the embattled camp with food and ammunition until the Communists were beaten back permanently. Initial runs with C-130s were dangerous because the runway was of insufficient length to accommodate the larger turboprop transports, so Navy Seabees were flown in to lengthen the strip. In the meantime, smaller

The Viet Cong assault against the American base at Khe Sanh near the Laos border in early 1968 was strongly reminiscent of the Vietminh assault against the French forces at Dienbienphu in 1954. The French defeat was the turning point in that conflict. But at Khe Sanh the Americans held, largely because of the massive air power available. Here an Air Force C-130 hastily unloads ammunition while under fire at Khe Sanh. (U.S. Air Force)

piston-engined C-123D Providers were called in to make supply runs. Savage combat in some areas, as well as hastily installed Communist antiaircraft guns, made the supply mission hazardous. The lumbering C-123Ds were easy targets for Viet Cong gunners and were often hit as they made their approach to the 3,900-foot runway at Khe Sanh. One Provider was downed, killing all forty-eight personnel on board.

The C-130s were also under constant attack. One Marine Hercules carrying a supply of helicopter fuel was hit by antiaircraft fire on February 11. An enemy .50-caliber bullet struck one of the bladders of fuel, which immediately ignited. In the resulting crash, of the eight crewmen only the two pilots survived.

Another Marine C-130 flown by Chief Warrant Officer Henry Wildfang was hit by enemy fire as it approached Khe Sanh on February 10 with a load of fuel. With over 15,000 flight hours, Wildfang was one of the last of that rare breed, the enlisted naval aviator. Having flown in three wars as both an officer and an enlisted man, Wildfang had to call upon all his experience to successfully land his crippled Hercules, its wings ablaze from Communist fire. As explosions rocked the lumbering Herk, Wildfang landed and maneuvered the transport off the runway to clear the way for those aircraft behind him. For his skill and courage, Wildfang was awarded his *fifth* DFC.

In an effort to more fully utilize the C-130's larger load capacity, the Air Force units flying some of the Hercules developed a method called "parachute extraction," whereby the transport never touched down, but flew low to the ground with its rear cargo ramp open. At a signal from the pilot, crewmen released the cargo pallets, along with an attached parachute which blossomed in the aircraft's slipstream and pulled the cargo out of the C-130. The system worked, but bulky cargo was difficult to drop safely, and the Marines on the ground were exposed to hostile fire if they had to retrieve items which rolled away from the main point of the drop.

Daily air support had become a way of life for the men on the ground; 1,600 sorties were flown by carrier aircraft in March alone, sometimes within 100 meters of American forces. It was clear that a more dynamic strategic air campaign had to be waged to dislodge the Viet Cong from around the base.

The Marines came up with their own system, which they called the "Super Gaggle," developed by the 1st Marine Air Wing. Intended to disrupt Viet Cong positions in the hills around Khe Sanh in order to allow supply operations to continue, the Super Gaggle involved the use of as many transport helicopters as could be mustered, with an escort of armed UH-1E Hueys and A-4s. Under the coordination of a TA-4F, circling above the action, the Gaggle would head out towards the camp, with the gunships and A-4s flying ahead, pounding the enemy positions with napalm and rockets. The transport helicopters, usually CH-46s, spiralled down through the clouds and mists which often overspread the area, deposited their supply loads, and took off again for bases at Da Nang and Chu Lai. The A-4s took advantage of orbiting KC-130 tankers to refuel and escort the empty helos back to safety.

Pummeled by strafing attacks, the Viet Cong nevertheless held on. Air Force tactical aircraft, such as the F-105, flew bombing missions, delivering a total of 35,000 tons of ordnance in the defense of Khe Sanh. The strike aircraft were aided by a system nicknamed "Combat Skyspot," which used radar aimed at the target from the ground. The director was then able to tell the approaching

Strategic bomber at war: USAF B-52D Stratofortress, designed to deliver four nuclear weapons against targets in the Soviet Union, unloads almost 30 tons of conventional "iron bombs" against suspected Viet Cong positions in South Vietnam. These giant planes, bombing through clouds with radar guidance, were highly effective in the benign environment over South Vietnam. When sent against targets in the North the situation would be far different. (U.S. Air Force)

aircraft when to release their bombs.

But it was Operation Arc Light, the ongoing use of huge B-52 strategic bombers in a tactical role, which finally evidently broke the enemy's resistance. The Stratofortresses had been in combat since 1965, operating from Guam. The big bombers were so successful that the United States pressed for permission to station them at the Royal Thai base at U-Tapao. The use of the base was granted and by July 1967, B-52s were operating regularly from Thailand in support of ground operations.

B-52s were called in to help in Khe Sanh, flying some 2,548 sorties and delivering nearly 60,000 tons of bombs, sometimes within 1,000 yards of Marine positions. General Westmoreland maintained later that the B-52 Arc Lights missions over Khe Sanh had broken the back of the Viet Cong effort.

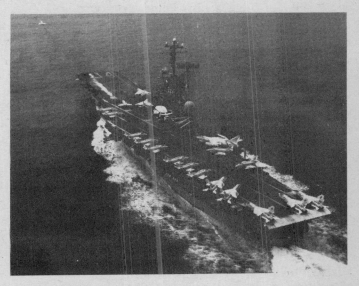

An A-4F Skyhawk goes off the No. 2 catapult of the *Oriskany* during a launch in the South China Sea. The dark rectangle on the starboard side of aft of the "island" is the deck-edge elevator swung to a vertical position, indicating that the ship recently has or will soon refuel from a fleet oiler. An EKA-3A Skywarrior parked next to the elevator dominates the flight deck. (U.S. Navy, R.A. Long)

The battle raged on for seventy-one days. As the monsoon rains and clouds began to dissipate in early April, Marine, Army and South Vietnamese Army units began Operation Pegasus, the rescue of Khe Sanh. But these men met surprisingly light resistance as they made their way through the various positions. The enemy had apparently dispersed under the heavy firepower of the Navy, Marine, and Air Force air strikes. Just as surprisingly, only four fixed-wing aircraft—a C-130, C-123, F-4, and A-4— were actually shot down in the fierce fighting, with seventeen helicopters also being destroyed.

In June, the decision was made to dismantle and destroy the base at Khe Sanh. Although the Communists loudly proclaimed a victory as Khe Sanh was abandoned, the United States merely pointed out that the base had served its purpose. The troops employed were essentially mobile anyway, and the time had come to leave.

BOMBING HALT AND REAPPRAISAL

While the big news from Vietnam during early 1968 revolved around the Communist offensive during Tet and the battle for Khe Sanh, major changes of an operational and political nature occurred by the time the siege at Khe Sanh was lifted in April. Foremost was the imposition by President Johnson of a so-called partial bombing halt which prohibited attacks north of the 20th parallel. This area, covering all but extreme southern North Vietnam, was so designed in an effort to motivate the Communists

208

Rain was constant day after day during the monsoon season in Southeast Asia. Here an E-2 Hawkeye AEW aircraft lands aboard the rain-swept deck of the *Coral Sea*. Parked at left is a soon-to-be-retired A-1 Skyraider, a pair of large A-3 Skywarriors, and a couple of A-4 Skyhawks—all Douglas-built aircraft designed by Ed Heinemann. (U.S. Navy)

for projected peace talks. Johnson had been under considerable pressure at home from those who wanted the United States to disengage from Vietnam and those who wished a sizeable reenforcement of American troops as a result of the Viet Cong attacks during Tet. There was also the upcoming Presidential election to consider; Johnson had announced that he would not seek re-election in November.

Johnson was finally convinced that reinforcement was not the answer, and that only a dialogue between the Communists, the South Vietnamese, and the Americans could resolve the conflict. In a mis-

Seemingly alone in the skies, an A-1H Skyraider from VA-25 aboard the *Coral Sea* heads for home. When this squadron went ashore in early 1968 it marked the end of the piston-engine fighter and attack aircraft in the fleet. The "Spad" flew in more than twenty major variants, probably more than any other combat aircraft. (U.S. Navy)

guided gesture of good faith, he therefore initiated the bombing halt, which relieved pressure on Hanoi and Haiphong — much to the pleasure and relief of the North Vietnamese. The situation can be compared, in some respects, with the Battle of Britain in 1940. Just at the moment when Luftwaffe bombing strikes and fighter sweeps seemed to be on the verge of bringing about the total collapse of the Royal Air Force defense, the Germans halted daylight operations over England, switching to night attacks, and postponing indefinitely their projected assault on Britain. The English were able to take advantage of the breathing space this "bombing halt" afforded them and reinforce their air defenses. The Germans had had the advantage and given it up. In the same way had the American policymakers, with the President at the head, given up the hard-won advantage to the Vietnamese in Hanoi. The United States had underestimated the Communists' courage and convictions, as well as their staying power.

Changes were also made in the inventory of the Navy's carrier aircraft. There were more A-7s, which had been proving to be capable attack aircraft, along with the retirement on April 10 of the A-1 Skyraider from the fleet. The last squadron to operate the A-1, VA-25 aboard the *Coral Sea*, relinquished its last aircraft during ceremonies at NAS Lemoore, California, after the carrier's return to the States. In a career spanning twenty-three years, the prop-driven Skyraider had flown in Korea as the major carrier attack aircraft, had been in service with Air Force squadrons since the beginning of Vietnam. In the latter war it had performed in a variety of roles, ranging from multi-seat electronic intelligence gathering to Navy antisubmarine warfare and rescue missions.

The skies of North Vietnam had proven too dangerous for the otherwise capable Skyraider, and the slower planes were largely relegated to missions in southern North Vietnam and South Vietnam itself. Often the strike force had to orbit, waiting for the Spads to catch up. The A-1s gave a good account of themselves in support of troops on the ground, in service as rescue coordinators, and even in encounters with MiGs; the A-1 was credited with two MiG-17s in aerial combat during its Vietnam service. The men who flew these last piston-engine attack planes were a breed apart, too. One A-1H pilot, in a colorful demonstration of elan, slid back his canopy as his plane was directed onto the catapult for a launch; while the deck crew connected the Skyraider up to the track, he unfurled a huge white scarf from around his neck. His ancient talisman fluttering in the slipstream, he and his plane were shot off into the air. In contrast to pilots of the new Navy aircraft, with multi-seats and multi-mission requirements, the pilots who flew the last A-1 missions in Vietnam had only themselves to rely on, and their large, slow, but dependable "Spads."

During the summer of 1968, with the partial bombing halt restricting attacks north, the A-7 Corsair squadrons aboard *Constellation* and *America* were kept busy flying missions in the southern panhandle region of North Vietnam and Laos. VA-27 and 97 in *Constellation* and VA-82 and 86 in *America* gained considerable combat experience with their A-7s. All four squadrons hit targets near Vinh in late September—bridges, barges, and storage depots, as well as SAM radar sites. The antiaircraft fire was intense, and several Corsairs were hit. The aircraft of VA-27's commanding officer sustained heavy damage over the target on a September 14 strike. With his starboard wing aflame, he managed to head out over the water and finally make Da Nang. However, as he approached the runway, the flames became too much and he ejected, the

Corsair crashing near a hangar. The pilot sustained only minor injuries and returned to his squadron the following day.

A-7s responded to several SAR efforts during this time. Two VA-82 pilots made repeated runs on enemy shore batteries on September 28, in order for the rescue helicopter to pick up a downed A-4 pilot from the *Hancock*. In August, a VA-27 pilot had been forced to eject from his crippled plane, landing only sixty yards offshore from Communist installations. The Communists were in the process of dispatching a small boat to capture the aviator when his squadron mates made runs on the boat, forcing its crew to abandon their craft. The HC-7 helo was able to pick up the VA-27 pilot.

The *Ticonderoga* brought two other A-7 equipped squadrons to the fighting, VA-25 and 87 with the first A-7Bs. The Corsair was demonstrating its ability to operate effectively from any carrier of the fleet, from the large *Constellation* and *America* to the World War II-era carriers like *Ticonderoga, Oriskany* and *Hancock*. *Constellation* and her air wing, CVW-14, were awarded the Meritorious Unit Commendation for their efforts during this period of intense activity.

MiG ACTIVITY — 1968

With the imposition of the March 31 bombing halt, the hunting ground for MiGs was considerably reduced. With only occasional reconnaissance flights by RF-8s and RA-5Cs, venturing into the

An F-4B Phantom from VF-154 aboard the carrier *Ranger* releases bombs over a Communist artillery position just north of the demilitarized zone in support of Marine operations to the south. Although on a bombing mission, the Phantom still carries Sidewinder air-to-air missiles to ward off MiG interceptors. A droptank is fitted on the plane's centerline pylons. (U.S. Navy, J.L. McDowell)

Hanoi/Haiphong area, MiG activity was sporadic. Sometimes radar would track MiGs coming south towards the Vinh area, the northernmost point to which American strikes could go. The MiGs would try to entice fighters into violating prohibited airspace, but the American pilots, under strict radar control and hindered by rules of engagement, would not play the game. In fact, the Air Force which had maintained such a high score, was able to rack up only eight kills during 1968, all of these within the January-February period prior to the bombing halt.

The Navy did no better, with the first Navy score not coming until June 26, when Commander Moose Meyers, commanding officer, of VF-51 from the *Bon Homme Richard*, shot down a MiG-21 while returning from an escort mission. Three kills were later gained in July, while August and September each saw one MiG downed. Most of the Navy's kills in 1968 were achieved by F-8s, which were flying from the smaller 27-Charlie-class carriers: the *Oriskany, Bon Homme Richard,* and *Hancock*. (The 27C ships were seven World War II *Essex*-class carriers — *Bon Homme Richard, Shangri-La, Hancock, Intrepid, Lexington, Ticonderoga,* and *Oriskany* — modified for jet operations in the 1950s.) The larger-deck ships always carried F-4 fighter squadrons.

The September 19th kill was of some significance, for it represented the last confirmed F-8 score of the Vietnam War. Lieutenant Anthony Nargi of VF-111 was part of a fighter detachment aboard the *Intrepid*. This unusual arrangement was necessary to provide protection for the smaller ASW carrier's attack unit. Nargi and his wingman were alerted to incoming MiGs and climbed to intercept the threat. The MiG-21s apparently spotted the F-8Cs and began evasive action. Nargi maneuvered his Crusader behind one of the MiGs and fired a Sidewinder. The missile tracked perfectly and blew the entire tail off the enemy fighter, as the North Vietnamese pilot ejected. The downed pilot's wingman then took on the two Americans, but although both F-8s fired missiles, no apparent damage was done and the second MiG escaped. This was the last kill for the F-8, which had been labeled as "Mig Master" by public-affairs officials. Officially, the Crusader shot down eighteen MiG-17s and 21s although a nineteenth kill was scored in May 1972 by a *Hancock*-based fighter. However, this unusual kill occurred as a result of the MiG pilot ejecting before the Crusaders which were pursuing him came within firing range. The Air Force had allowed several kills during the course of the war which were apparently obtained through the use of "maneuvering." The Navy was less generous, and this particular kill was not credited to a pilot.

AIRCRAFT CHANGES

The Marines gained a new and much needed aircraft when the first North American OV-10 Broncos arrived at Da Nang on July 6, 1968. The long-awaited LARA (Light Armed Reconnaissance Aircraft) was the result of a 1962 Marine Corps study on small, lightly armed aircraft for use in counter-insurgency (COIN) operations. The Defense Department took an official interest and soon companies were invited to submit proposals for the new airplane. Eleven companies responded, with North American's design finally winning the production contract. Production for the Marines and Air Force began in 1966. While the Marines took actual delivery of its first Bronco in February 1968, the first aircraft did not arrive in South Vietnam until July; but little time was lost in introducing the plane into operations.

The classic OV-10A Bronco in flight over Southeast Asian waters. The North American-built plane was developed specifically for counterinsurgency (COIN). Although configured to serve as a mini-transport and medical evacuation aircraft, the OV-10As operated mainly as attack and reconnaissance aircraft in South Vietnam's skies. (U.S. Navy, R. Blair)

A pair of OV-10A aircraft from Navy Light Attack Squadron [VAL) 4 close up before a firing run over a Viet Cong position. The planes are armed with rockets mounted on wing and fuselage pylons. The after end of the fuselage could be opened to carry a couple of troops or stretchers. (U.S. Navy, A.R. Hill)

A rocket-armed OV-10A Bronco takes off from Vung Tau in South Vietnam. The OV-10A is a STOL (Short Take-Off and Landing) aircraft, and subsequently the planes have operated from helicopter carriers without the use of catapults or arresting gear. (U.S. Navy, A.R. Hill)

The same two OV-10A aircraft from VAL-4 search out the enemy in the Rung Sat area of South Vietnam. The aircraft's design is reminiscent of two famed World War II twin-boom aircraft, the P-38 Lightning and P-61 Black Widow fighters. The Marine Corps flew five of the latter after the war as the F2T-1. (U.S. Navy, A.R. Hill)

Looking like a World War II fighter with its twin tail-booms and three-bladed propellors, the OV-10 began operations with VMO-2 at Marble Mountain, with a second Marine unit, VMO-6 equipping by October. OV-10As were used as slow-speed mission coordinators during helicopter operations; while A-4s and F-4s protected the main helo forces, the Broncos maintained watch over the mission as an airborne scout. Armed with rockets and gun pods, the Broncos were ideally suited for troop suppression and reconnaissance flights in advance of troop movements.

The Navy acquired OV-10s in 1971 to equip a special squadron, designated VAL-4 (Light Attack Squadron). Nicknamed the "Black Ponies," VAL-4 served along side HAL-3, which operated UH-1 Hueys. The two units were tasked with providing protection for river convoys along the Mekong River in South Vietnam, as well as supporting operations on the ground. With a 20-mm gun pod mounted on the fuselage centerline station, and various rocket pods on the stub-wings beneath the fuselage, the Navy Broncos began operations on February 28, 1971, eventually becoming the last Navy unit in Vietnam in April 1971.

Another Navy aircraft left the inventory when the last P-5 Marlin was retired in July, ending an era in naval aviation. The Martin aircraft was the last operational seaplane in the Navy, and had served the U.S. fleet for sixteen years, as well as serving in the French Aeronavale. Several squadrons had used the twin-engined flying boat during early Market Time missions.

AERIAL RECONNAISSANCE

The importance of aerial reconnaissance in Vietnam cannot be overstressed. It often was the only means of knowing the status of enemy forces and supply routes. Of all the so-called "support" missions—those not directly responsible for delivering ordnance or control of the air—photo reconnaissance was perhaps the most dangerous because the aircraft usually employed (the RF-8A/G Crusader, RA-5C Vigilante, or RA-3B Skywarrior) was unarmed, and its pilot had to rely on speed and skill to evade enemy defenses. The reconnaissance contingents suffered a casualty rate out of proportion to their size.

At no time was the need for reconnaissance more strongly demonstrated than during the Christmas truce periods, especially of 1967–68 prior to the Tet offensive, and after the November 1, 1968 bombing halt. While most of the American forces enjoyed a holiday standdown, the photographic detachments were working hard.

As has been noted earlier, reconnaissance flights were the earliest form of American participation in Vietnam. RF-8A dets aboard U.S. carriers, including some Marine RF-8As, flew a number of intelligence-gathering missions over Vietnam and Laos. Indeed, the photo-Crusaders had been so active over the northern areas in late 1964 that it was with some amusement that Lieutenant (j.g.) Richard Coffman, watched a senior fighter pilot's reaction upon learning he would be flying over the north as escort to the junior man's RF-8A. In disbelief, the

An RA-3B Skywarrior shows off its camera lens. This version of the venerable "Whale" had twelve camera stations plus stowage for extra film, and an arsenal of flash bombs for night photography. The plane was flown by a crew of three: pilot, photo-navigator-assistant pilot, and photo technician. Note the carrier arresting hook retracted into the tail. (U.S. Navy, C. Larson)

Lieutenant Commander asked if the younger pilot was sure, saying the fighter squadrons had no idea that the photobirds were flying so far north. Coffman assured him that the route was accurate and that it was actually a routine hop.

As with many of the tactical military air operations in Vietnam, the proper prosecution of the war was hindered by bureaucracy as well as uncertainty. The reconnaissance units of the Navy were also affected; many RF-8s were lost because the North Vietnamese could predict their routines.

While perhaps grimly humorous, the following incident illustrates what could happen if the predictability of recon flights was altered. An RF-8G and its escort F-4B were launched from the *Coral Sea* to take post-strike photography of a mission against the fabled Thanh Hoa Bridge in 1968. The bomber force hit the bridge amidst a barrage of antiaircraft fire. Within a predictable minute or two of the strike force's departure, the photo pilot made his run over the target, meeting the same heavy fire, this time concentrating on one aircraft.

Finishing his run, the Crusader pilot rejoined the Phantom which had stood off to intercept possible MiG threats to the RF-8, as well as to provide instant air cover should the recon plane be shot down. The photo pilot, Lieutenant (j.g.) Jay Miller, cleared his throat and informed his escort pilot, Lieutenant Commander Pete Purvis, that he had "a problem or two," and that it was necessary to refly the run. In reality, Miller, an experienced aviator, had forgotten to turn on his camera switches, and had not gotten any coverage of the target. Since the strike was of special interest to the carrier group commander, coverage was mandatory; however, there were fuel considerations, as well as the thought of flying back through the flak area. Nevertheless, the RF-8 driver turned around and hastily flew over the bridge once more, getting the necessary photography. Amazingly, no flak rose toward him. The reason was obvious: the people on the ground were not expecting the photobird to make a second run, and so had relaxed their vigilance. Obviously, if other reconnaissance pilots had been allowed to vary their individual times over the target, especially after a large strike, many men would have been recovered safely aboard their carriers instead of being lost, or becoming prisoners of war.

The RF-8A/G Crusaders made up what was termed the "light" photographic community of the Navy, while the "heavy" equipment consisted of RA-5C Vigilantes and RA-3B Skywarriors. The RA-5C was a development of the A-5A carrier-based Mach 2 bomber of the late 1950s. Trouble with the novel bomb bay, as well as changes in the Navy's strategic missions, eliminated the need for a supersonic heavy bomber. Instead, the Vigilante was modified to carry more fuel and to carry an innovative "canoe" filled with photographic and infrared sensors fitted beneath the fuselage.

RVAH-5 became the first squadron to use the Vigilante in combat during the *Ranger*'s 1964–65 deployment to Vietnam. During these early phases of the war, the development of attack routes, especially for the incoming A-6s, was an important task and the RA-5Cs were instrumental in gaining the necessary photographs to plan these routes.

The Vigilante operated only from so-called "big deck" carriers, not only because of its size, but because the airplane was part of the total reconnaissance system, the Integrated Operational Intelligence Center (IOIC), installed only in the larger

A camouflaged RA-3B Skywarrior and its twelve cameras rest on the runway at Guam before a flight to Southeast Asia. Guam was a staging point for the Navy and the operating base for Air Force B-52s, with the latter also operating out of Thailand. Thirty "Whales" were delivered to the Navy in the RA-38 configuration (originally A3D-2P). The twin-20mm cannon originally fitted in the tail of this aircraft have been replaced by electronic equipment. (U.S. Navy)

ships such as the *Forrestal* class. This system involved new interpretative machinery and procedures, all of which produced photographic prints within ten minutes of the aircraft's return to the carrier. At its peak, the RA-5C equipped ten squadrons, all but two of which made combat deployments to Vietnam.

RA-5Cs suffered a comparatively high casualty rate in combat, again because of their predictability over the target areas. But the Vigilante also had its enemies on the Navy side. The aircraft's expensive sophistication made it somewhat of an unknown quantity, as well as a maintenance nightmare for squadron and carrier skippers alike. It was the old

An RA-5C "Viggie" is catapulted from the carrier *Ranger* for a reconnaissance mission over North Vietnam. Developed from the A-5 (A3J) supersonic strike aircraft, the RA-5C variant carried five camera systems plus Side-Looking Aircraft Radar (SLAR) and Electronic Countermeasures (ECM) equipment. Weapons could still be carried internally or on wing pylons, but the aircraft were employed in Vietnam only in the recce role. (U.S. Navy, Donald Granthan)

story of "when she was good, she was very, very good, but when she was bad, she was horrid." When the Vigilante's systems worked and were tasked properly, it was the best tactical photo reconnaissance platform in the Navy, perhaps in the military service. But the immediacy of military tactical requirements was sometimes against the RA-5C. Its camera systems needed special preparation and warmup procedures which could not be varied, and many times the less temperamental RF-8 filled in for its larger brother.

A black RA-3B from Heavy Photographic Squadron (VAP) 61 comes aboard a carrier in Southeast Asian waters after a nighttime flight over enemy territory. (U.S. Navy)

A Navy-flown EC-121 Warning Star similar to this aircraft was shot down over international waters in April 1969 by the North Koreans. The large, land-based military version of the Lockheed Constellation was used for electronic surveillance, with the ventral and belly domes housing AN/APS-20 and -45 search radars. (U.S. Navy)

Enlisted photographic intelligence specialists aboard the carrier *Bon Homme Richard* plot enemy locations for possible air strikes. Earlier these men had scrutinized aerial photographs of the terrain to identify the enemy positions. Like many other men aboard the carriers, the intelligence personnel worked long hours before and after the strikes of the day were flown. (U.S. Navy, C.B. Winther)

However, the RA-5C flew throughout the Vietnam War with distinction. On June 6, 1967, an RVAH-7 Vigilante from the *Enterprise* brought back coverage of an area southwest of Hanoi. Close examination of the pictures revealed a well-camouflaged SAM site with ten missiles. Next morning, the first strike from the carrier hit the site, catching missiles in launchers and transporters. Pilots reported seeing missiles exploding in their cradles and skimming along the ground in wild erratic maneuvers as their fuel was ignited by the bombs. An RVAH-7 Vigilante followed the strike force to take damage photography, sustaining a AAA hit right beneath the pilot's position.

This story also illustrates another side of the reconnaissance mission. In most military aircraft squadrons, there are certain ground personnel, officer and enlisted, who can generally be listed as intelligence specialists. In tactical units, those squadrons tasked with weapons delivery — fighters and attack aircraft — are largely responsible for providing current information concerning enemy air and ground threats, target layouts, and day-to-day news items of interest to the flight crews. However, the intelligence personnel of a reconnaissance squadron, in addition to those duties, also have another primary function: photo interpretation.

When a reconnaissance pilot returns to the carrier, his plane's film is rushed to the intelligence spaces for developing. When the film is developed, a process just as important as flying of the mission, itself, is performed: the debrief. Working closely with the pilot, the intelligence officer and enlisted specialist go over the newly developed negatives on a light table. With his mission still fresh in his mind, the pilot literally reflies the route as he looks at the negatives, noting items of interest for the specialists: new construction, SAM sites, trucks, or changes in normal patterns on the ground. The interpreters can then gain specific knowledge concerning the mission, and can annotate subsequent prints of individual frames for inclusion into the mission planning and policy-making process. It is this close working relationship which sets the reconnaissance community apart from other tactical squadrons, and led to the overall success of the reconnaissance mission over Vietnam.

Yet, for all the impact which reconnaissance squadrons had in the day-to-day conduct of the war, a career as a reconnaissance pilot in the Navy was not the best path for advancement. No RF-8 pilot who stayed within the light photo-reconnaissance community was given command of an air group, and only a select few of the RA-5C flight crews reached that position. VFP detachments aboard carriers were normally commanded by no higher rank than a lieutenant commander, while the larger fighter and attack (VF and VA, respectively) squadrons were led by full commanders; the air wings counted senior commanders and junior captains at their head. Even though he had charge of what amounted to a small squadron, with its accompanying responsibilities, the officer-in-charge of a photo detachment was still a junior officer in charge of a support group and was not in the right pipeline for command.

The field of motion-picture photography was also explored, cameras being installed in the RA-5C and A-4, the latter aircraft having much greater success. The RA-5's installation was an improvised affair which took up precious film space. The A-4's camera, installed along the centerline, provided a forward view of the aircraft's flight path and was comparatively easy to maintain.

Enterprise was the next carrier to be hit by a major fire, on January 14, 1969. The big ship was steaming off Hawaii for an exercise prior to returning to Vietnam, when a Zuni rocket on an F-4 was accidentally ignited during startup procedures. Within a few minutes, the blaze had reached major proportions and General Quarters was sounded, sending all personnel to assigned stations. Within three hours the fire was under control, and extinguished, but twenty-eight men had died and fifteen aircraft had been destroyed; losses were more than 56 million dollars.

Repairs to the nuclear carrier were made at Pearl Harbor, and *Enterprise* left Hawaii for the western Pacific on June 26, eventually arriving on Yankee Station on October 8, after a stopover in the Philippines and Indian Ocean areas. By February four carriers were on the line: *Hancock, Kitty Hawk, Ranger*, and *Coral Sea*, with *Hancock* leaving by mid-month. Corsair II squadrons were especially active during this period. VA-37 and 105 in the *Kitty Hawk* and VA-25 and 87 in *Ticonderoga* attacked troop camps, supply routes, and storage areas in South Vietnam. On February 15, VA-105 aircraft dropped 2,000-pound bombs on a storage area south of Hue, the old Vietnamese imperial capital.

In April, the North Koreans took on American resolve again, shooting down an EC-121 electronic surveillance aircraft; the entire thirty-one-man crew was lost over international waters. Task Force 71 of

The *Enterprise* was the third aircraft carrier to be struck by tragedy during the Vietnam War. The giant carrier was steaming off Hawaii on exercises on January 14, 1969 when a rocket accidently ignited, setting off a series of devastating explosions. When it was over twenty-eight men were dead and the after end of the flight deck heavily damaged. According to Navy statements, in an emergency the ship could have continued flight operations a few hours after the fires were extinguished. (U.S. Navy)

Pueblo fame was reactivated, again with *Enterprise* as the flagship, and reentered North Korean waters. P-3s found debris of the downed plane, and destroyers recovered a few of the bodies. The President ordered resumption of reconnaissance flights over the Sea of Japan soon after the incident. By the end of April, after a suitable show of force, the task force had been reduced to eight ships from the

Fires extinguished, the *Enterprise* steams toward Pearl Harbor with the charred remains of fifteen aircraft scattered around her after flight deck. Several holes in the armored deck mark where bombs under aircraft had exploded. (U.S. Navy, Stanley C. Wyckoff)

high point of twenty-nine vessels, including four carriers on April 21.

MARINE PROGRESS

April 1969 also saw the introduction of Bell Huey Cobras into Marine service, the first AH-1Gs operating with VMO-2 at Marble Mountain. Developed by Bell as a private venture, the slim little Huey Cobra was a designed-for-the-purpose helicopter gunship, offering a slim profile for enemy gunners to aim at, as well as a variety of weapon possibilities. Originally powered by a single Lycoming turboshaft engine, the AH-1G was developed into the twin-engined, Pratt and Whitney-powered AH-1J model, expressly for the Marines who found the modification essential for overwater operation. The new helicopters were used not only for escort and fire control missions, but also armed reconnaissance. The new AH-1J appeared in 1971 and was used by the Marines during the Laotian incursion, Lam Son 719, escorting the larger CH-53 transport helicopters.

The Bell AH-1J SeaCobra, designed specifically for the Marine Corps, was ordered into production in May 1968. Although the Cobra's fuselage was radically different than that of the basic "Huey," the AH-1G had the earlier helicopter's engine, transmission, and rotor system. A three-barrel 20-mm gun is mounted in the chin turret and rocket pods are carried on the stub wings. (U.S. Marine Corps, S. Powell)

Marine helicopters, as described previously, had been in the vanguard of American participation in Vietnamese combat operations. The first airborne contingents had been Marine UH-34s and elderly CH-37 Mojaves, which were the largest helicopter available at that time. However, by the 1966–67 period, helicopter operations had become more complex, and involved an increasing number of different aircraft to accomplish a variety of missions: transport, reconnaissance, fire support, and escort protection. The largest helicopter used was the big Sikorsky CH-53D Sea Stallion, which entered service in 1969, offering more power and performance than earlier models of the CH-53. The CH-53 had entered Marine squadrons in late 1966, replacing the CH-37 Mojave as the heavy transport helicopter.

The CH-46 augmented and then replaced the workhorse UH-34 as the main transport helicopter. Lieutenant Colonel E. R. Brady, the commanding officer of HMM-364, earned the Navy Cross for the May 15, 1969 action in which he brought his helicopter into a battle zone to pick up eight seriously wounded Marines. With darkness fast approaching, and the weather rapidly deteriorating, he landed his aircraft under intense enemy fire from only thirty yards away. Waiting for the troops to board his helicopter, Lieutenant Colonel Brady relayed the enemy positions to orbiting fixed-wing aircraft, and then finally lifted his CH-46 out of the landing zone, amidst heavy mortar fire.

Some idea of the intensity of helicopter operations can be gained from the number of medevac sorties during the peak year of 1968. In that single year, 42,000 helicopter missions were flown with some 67,000 people rescued.

8

The Withdrawal Begins

Despite the partial halt in air strikes, the Communists continued to press the attack in South Vietnam. In an effort to silence criticism at home, and to further encourage the Communists to negotiate, President Johnson, in his last major decision of the war, instituted a complete bombing halt of North Vietnam to commence on November 1. The last mission north of the DMZ was credited to the Commander of Air Wing Fourteen aboard the *Constellation*, who flew a VA-97 Corsair II on a bridge-busting mission.

President Richard M. Nixon returned the Republicans to the White House in January 1969. His election to the presidency came after several years of intense U.S. involvement in Vietnam. There were American ground troops in South Vietnam, plus massive U.S. naval and air forces supporting them in Thailand, the Philippines, and Guam, with the mighty U.S. Seventh Fleet offshore. But perhaps one of the strongest factors in the war had become the noisy and sometimes violent public domestic outcry against American participation. Massive demonstrations in Washington, D.C. and several large American cities had inhibited the Johnson Administration from taking any decisive steps towards a military solution to the war. With the North Vietnamese seemingly unafraid of the American power arrayed against them, and the resulting stalemate, the incoming Nixon Administration was faced with very few alternatives. Large-scale withdrawal was the path chosen.

Throughout the first half of 1969, air operations concentrated in South Vietnam in observance of the bombing halt imposed the preceding November, centering mainly in the so-called I Corps area, immediately south of the DMZ. However, June 5 saw strikes into North Vietnam in retaliation for the shooting down of an RF-8 reconnaissance Crusader. To safely conduct reconnaissance missions, armed escorts, A-4 Iron Hand anti-SAM aircraft, an A-4 RESCAP, available Marine radar jammers, and Navy tankers were all tasked with protecting the photobird. The need for reconnaissance aircraft was so great during this period that the production line for the RA-5C was reopened for the manufacture of forty-six additional aircraft, bringing the total number of Vigilantes produced to 140. RF-8s were also included in the program, including the RF-8A of Major John H. Glenn, number 144608, which the famous Marine astronaut (and Senator) flew in his 1957 transcontinental flight. Glenn's Crusader was modified to RF-8G standards and issued to VFP-63, but was eventually lost off the *Oriskany* in 1973.

VFP-63, the fleet light photo squadron, was also given an additional responsibility and equipment when F-8H fighters were transferred to the photo unit. The idea was to enable the various detachments of VFP-63 to provide their own fighter escorts, which had previously been the responsibility of accompanying fighter squadrons serving with the air wings. The idea, although theoretically promising, did not pan out, and with the continuing need for fighter F-8s by the other squadrons, the Hs were finally returned to the fighter squadrons. (However, VFP-63 eventually regained its fighter complement, as the F-8 left fleet service in 1974, and several Crusader-equipped squadrons were disbanded or re-equipped with more modern equipment.)

As the war continued in the south, with minor incursions into the North, American policy began a new tack when President Nixon announced on June 8, during a meeting with South Vietnamese President Thieu, that he was ordering a phased withdrawal of American troops. Twenty-five-thousand men were recalled from South Vietnam by August 29. Over the next year over 100,000 troops were pulled out of South Vietnam fighting.

The carriers remained on station. In July, 1,025 sorties were flown by carrier aircraft in the I Corps area. In September, F-8s from the *Hancock* flew support missions in support of the First Marine Division, southwest of Da Nang.

In August, the North Vietnamese unexpectedly released three prisoners of war, including a pilot of

With afterburner flaming, an RF-8 Photo Crusader of VFP-63 takes off from a land base. Naval aircraft are equally at home afloat or ashore. The "PP" tail marking shows this aircraft is under operational control of the parent squadron and not assigned to a specific carrier air wing, at which time it would take on the wing's tail code. (U.S. Navy)

VF-151 who had been shot down along with his commanding officer on October 24, 1967, flying from the *Coral Sea*. Lieutenant Robert Frishman confirmed American fears when he reported brutal treatment of American POWs by the North Vietnamese. Frishman and his skipper had been brought down during a strike against Haiphong, the two planes being hit by SAMs directly over the city during the intense bombing action.

After a sixteen-month interlude, an American aircraft downed a MiG when an F-4J of VF-142 from the *Constellation* shot down a MiG-21 on March 28, 1970, during a photo escort mission. This was to be the only American kill for the next two years. There had been much speculation by Navy pilots on the reluctance of the MiGs to appear

240

The *Shangri-La* (CVS-38) served one combat tour in Southeast Asia, from April to November 1970, operating F-8E Crusaders from VF-111 and VF-162 shown here.

In-flight refueling by carrier-based tanker aircraft increased combat ranges or payloads, and saved many damaged aircraft that would otherwise have not reached a carrier or airfield ashore. In these two photos one EKA-3B "Whale" assigned to a VAH-4 detachment aboard the carrier *Hancock* refuels another "Whale" from the ship over the South China Sea. (U.S. Navy)

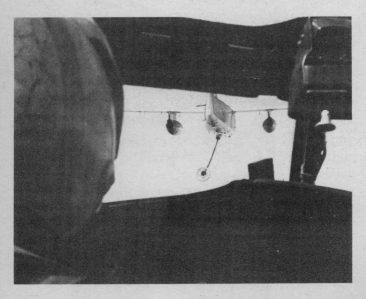

after the bombing halt, especially when the American fighter involved was the Crusader. (There had always been a fierce, but friendly rivalry between F-8 and F-4 flight crews, concerning the single- versus two-seat advantages of each aircraft, as well as the fixed-gun armament of the F-8 as opposed to the all-missile arrangement of the Phantom.) The VF-142 kill, coming three days after the F-8-equipped *Hancock* had left the line, seemed to bear out the feeling of many Crusader pilots that the MiG pilots would rather engage F-4s rather than F-8s. Indeed, the previously mentioned "kill" in May 1972 by two F-8s from the *Hancock* provided some interesting radio transmissions by the North Vietnamese pilot prior to his ejecting from his MiG before either of the American fighters had fired a shot. His ground controller had evidently told the oncoming MiG that his opposition would be two F-4s; however upon gaining visual contact, the pilot was heard to say something to the effect that the controller had been quite mistaken and that the American bogies were, in fact, F-8s. He bailed out of his plane soon afterwards. Of course, the meaning of this is open to discussion. But the North Vietnamese were probably concentrating their resources towards Air Force raids, rather than engaging Navy BARCAP fighters. F-8 squadron plans to entice MiGs down south were not successful, even when the lure was big B-52 Arc Light raids; elaborate "pincer" movements set up by the frustrated Crusader drivers went untried.

The new year saw the war continue in much the same vein as in the previous twelve months, but the

As the venerable "Whales" were phased out of the fleet, the in-flight refueling role was taken over by specifically configured KA-6D Intruders. Here a prototype Intruder tanker refuels an A-6A attack aircraft from VA-42 during flight tests. (Grumman)

phased withdrawal program was becoming a hard fact, at least for the ground forces. Marine aviation was also reduced as several fighter and attack squadrons returned to Japan and the United States. Even the important base at Chu Lai was vacated by the Marines and turned over to the U.S. Army in October.

The veteran carrier *Bon Homme Richard*, after completing its record sixth combat deployment in November, was scheduled for decommissioning by mid-1971, leaving *Oriskany* and *Hancock* as the only 27C carriers in combat. *Oriskany* made her fifth Vietnam cruise with two Corsair squadrons, VAs 153 and 155, replacing three previous Skyhawk squadrons.

NEW EQUIPMENT AND MODELS

Corsair development entered a new phase when the first A-7Es deployed in *America* with VA-147, the first squadron to use the A-7A in combat. The E model featured greater weapons delivery accuracy and a Rolls Royce/Allison turbofan engine. The first combat missions were flown on May 23, and pilots were enthusiastic about the new A-7. The A-7E was particularly active at night along the Ho Chi Minh Trail. Fitted with a Heads-Up Display (HUD), the Echo enabled the pilot to concentrate on his mission without diverting his eyes to his instruments.

The *America* also brought two new models of the A-6 Intruder to the combat zone, the A-6C and the tanker KA-6D. The A-6C featured a development called TRIM, for Trails, Roads, Interdiction Multi-sensor, which incorporated large wing-mounted pods with electro-optical sensors. The A-6C employed a video-display which denoted the presence of targets along supply routes.

The KA-6D, which represented a new generation of carrier-borne refueling aircraft, was limited to a 3-g load, and therefore was not able to perform a secondary attack mission. The A-4 and A-3 remained the primary refueling platforms.

The big A-3 had always performed as the primary air-to-air tanker, and many carrier pilots owed their successful return to the orbiting Whale which flew between the beach and the ship, waiting to provide damaged aircraft with much-needed fuel. A procedure was developed out of Vietnam combat which was aptly called "wet-winging." A heavily damaged A-4 had made its way to the water, fuel streaming from its ruptured tanks. Finding the A-3 tanker, the Skyhawk pilot plugged in, and the two aircraft flew back to the carrier, the tanker feeding JP-4 continuously to the struggling A-4 as it approached the deck. Finally, just before touchdown, the A-4 disconnected and landed safely. Wet-winging became a standard procedure for damaged planes returning to the carrier.

ACTION IN CAMBODIA AND LAOS

The ongoing problem of Viet Cong infiltration and encampments in Cambodia finally forced the Cambodian government to seek American aid, especially after a March 18 coup which deposed Prince Sihanouk while he was in Moscow trying to get the Russians to reduce activity in his country. General Lon Nol, upon taking over the reins of the government, asked for American help and by April 29 a full-scale invasion of Cambodia was under way, with Allied forces spearheaded by South Vietnamese units. The campaign, which brought storms of protest from antiwar groups in the United States, was unable to stem the Communist control over Cambodia, and they continued to use the country as a base of operations against the south.

It had been made patently clear by the November 1, 1968 bombing halt that Rolling Thunder was a failure. The announced intention of hindering Communist efforts and eventually bringing them to the peace table had not been realized. However, with the bombing halt in the North, operations did not cease. In fact, the bombing did not stop or even diminish. It was merely transferred across the Annamite mountains to focus on the infiltration corridors running through Laos. The various supply trails which made up the Ho Chi Minh Trail had always been prime targets for both day and night operations. Much effort had been made to cope with the special problems presented by the twisting, heavily camouflaged jungle trails and roads by which the Viet Cong moved their complex supply system to the southern areas. With the end of the Rolling Thunder campaign, the Defense Department recommended that concentrated operations begin against this supply network as it filtered through Laos.

Various electronic sensors, similar to those which had served so well during the 1968 siege of Khe Sanh, were dropped by various aircraft, from F-4s to helicopters, along the trails to monitor enemy traffic. Operating from the base at Nakhon Phanom, known as "Naked Fanny" to the troops stationed there, in Thailand, special Navy OP-2E Neptunes of VO-67 sowed fields of "Spikebuoy" and "Adsid" acoustical sensors which buried themselves two-and-one-half feet into the ground and listened for seismic disturbances along the trails, including vehicular and foot traffic. Clandestine monitoring was essential to the interdiction effort. One Air Force officer said later during the daytime, the Ho Chi Minh trails were deceptively deserted and ". . . unless you were a fully trained observer, you would say it was a deserted road . . . But that night I flew over again and saw 200 trucks coming into Laos with their lights on." "Most of the North Vietnamese trucks had American planes flying above them thirty percent of the time they were in Laos . . ." The same officer recounted an extreme measure wherein a helicopter was outfitted with various blinking lights and sirens, which somehow gave the impression of a dragon stalking the jungle trails. Evidently the disguise worked to some extent, even better than bombs, in discouraging the truck drivers.

A stronger measure was the gunship. Normally peaceful transport aircraft, they were given sophisticated radar suites, outfitted with banks of rapid-fire mini-guns, and sent out at night to interdict the trails. The older AC-47, AC-123K, and AC-119K gunships found a new role as they orbited concentrations of trucks, creating their own miniature hells with concentrated machine-gun fire. The newer AC-130A was the most powerful gunship, carrying 7.62-mm miniguns, 105-mm howitzers and 40- and 20-mm cannon.

SPECIAL OPERATIONS

Some idea of the unusual methods employed during the campaign along the Ho Chi Minh Trail can be obtained by looking at the activities of VO-67. Observation Squadron 67, with its highly modified Lockheed Neptunes, was such an unusual unit that it merits special attention. Enemy infiltration along the various roads and paths of the larger Ho Chi Minh Trail was so intense that Secretary of Defense McNamara in the fall of 1966 requested the Army propose additional methods of dealing with

One of the most unusual uses of naval aircraft in the Vietnam War was the employment of OP-2E Neptunes in Navy Observation Squadron (VO) 67 to monitor Communist supply and troop movements into South Vietnam. This OP-2E at rest shows the sensor dispenser installed in its tail in place of the traditional MAD "stinger" and the camera pod under the rear fuselage. (U.S. Navy)

the flow of men and material from North Vietnam. The Army submitted a plan calling for the emplacement of seismic and acoustical sensors along the trails to detect traffic. Although the Army's plan was accepted, it would be another year until the system could be developed for planting with the proposed Air Force F-4 Phantoms. The Navy was tasked with the creation of a squadron to fill the gap.

As McNamara wanted the Navy unit operational by November 15, 1967, events moved rapidly—so rapidly, in fact, that at the squadron's commissioning ceremony on February 15, 1967, only twenty-three officers and enlisted men were on hand. Most of the additional complement was still in transit and training. Initial training, carried out under the auspices of VP-31, included survival and escape courses, counterinsurgency indoctrination and aircraft familiarization.

The aircraft which VO-67 was to operate was the veteran Lockheed P-2 Neptune, long the backbone of the maritime patrol squadrons of the Navy, as well as several allied countries. The model chosen for the squadron was the SP-2E, but with the large amount of internal and external modifications needed to outfit the plane for the squadron's mission, the aircraft was redesignated OP-2E. These major external modifications, which were conducted by Martin Aircraft in Baltimore, Maryland, included: the removal of the distinctive Magnetic Anomoly Detection (MAD) tailboom to allow the introduction of chaff dispensers; the removal of the wingtip tanks; the addition of two SUU-11 7.62-mm mini-gun pod under each wing; the provision of internally mounted cameras; and fiberglass propellers. These propellers caused maintenance problems during subsequent operations, with 80 percent of the propellers changed during deployment due to damage from runway debris.

Internally, the Neptunes were also substantially altered. All ASW equipment was deleted and self-sealing fuel tanks installed. A chaff system and various radios were introduced, as well as a Norden bombsight to direct sensor emplacements, and provision for M-60 hand-held 7.62-mm guns in waist positions. Painted in a dark jungle-green camouflage, the "chopped and blocked" P-2s took on a sinister appearance in keeping with their highly secretive missions.

With the arrival of additional squadron personnel, bringing the total roster to 300, VO-67 left its base at Alameda, California, and arrived at Nakhon Phanom Royal Thai Air Force base on the target date of November 15, 1967. The disproportionate amount of senior members made the squadron's rank structure top-heavy. The commanding officer was a captain, with eleven commanders and five lieutenant commanders. There were also twenty-three chief petty officers in the enlisted ranks. The heavy seniority was necessary, it was felt, to offset the lack of time for training and familiarization for the squadron. The senior pilots would be able to mold their crews into working units more quickly.

Nakhon Phanom was the home for several Air Force units, including HH-3 SAR helicopters, the colorful "Sandy" A-1E, A-1H Skyraiders which provided protection for SAR operations, World War II-vintage A-26 trial-interdiction aircraft, and Cessna O-2 FAC aircraft. Space on the base was so cramped that the new arrivals of VO-67 were forced to conduct maintenance on the ramps in the open, without benefit of hangars. However, at that time the Nakhon Phanom base did have the following facilities: officer's open mess, NCO club, airmen's dining hall, base exchange, chapel, swimming pool, base theater, hobby shops, base library, and University of Maryland Extension Courses, plus a six-lane bowling alley under construction, in addition to barracks for the several thousand U.S. troops.

Modifications continued through January 1968,

with the OP-2Es being equipped with terrain avoidance radar and a specialized LORAN navigational system. By February 2, 1968, all twelve Neptunes had been through the rotational mod program at Sangley Point in Philippines, and squadron assets were at peak levels.

The squadron flew its first operational mission on November 25, 1967, and within a month had suffered its first battle damage. The first aircraft losses came in fairly rapid succession. On January 11, 1968, the Neptune carrying the squadron's Executive Officer, Commander D. A. Olsen, and his crew of eight, failed to return from a mission. The wreckage of Olsen's plane was located at the base of a cliff two weeks later. It was determined that the plane had flown into the cliff in bad weather, while climbing out after dropping its sensors.

The next loss, directly attributed to combat action, occurred on February 17, when another plane was hit by AAA while dropping sensors from an altitude of only 500 feet. Escorting Phantoms called the VO-67 pilot to tell him his starboard engine was on fire. Climbing back into the cloud layer above him, the pilot acknowledged, saying he was returning to Nakhon Phanom and that he was "pretty beat up," which indicated further battle damage. However, three minutes later, the orbiting FAC in a O-2 reported sighting burning wreckage in the jungle along the Neptune's flight path. All nine crewmen had perished.

By this time, it was apparent that the lumbering P-2s, like their prop-driven contemporaries, the A-1s, could not survive in areas of antiaircraft concentration. On February 18, a conference was convened to discuss the means of decreasing the OP-2E's vulnerability to ground fire.

As if to underscore the problem, the squadron's third combat loss occurred on February 27, when a Neptune was shot down during an emplacement mission over Laos. The plane had flown into a hornet's nest of 37-mm antiaircraft fire and one projectile had smashed through the fuselage, killing an enlisted crewman instantly and starting a fire which filled the aircraft with flames and smoke. The aircraft commander, flying from the right seat at the time, immediately ordered his men to bail out. The eight surviving crewmen jumped; seven were rescued by helicopter, but the aircraft commander, one of the last to leave the plane, was never found. Several other aircraft sustained hits from ground fire, and in one case, only the provision of self-sealing gas tanks prevented another loss.

The conference on the OP-2E's vulnerability made several recommendations, including a limitation to one pass over the target areas, alternative target areas, minimum weather requirements, and the suggestion that the use of smoke markers from accompanying FAC aircraft be reduced, especially if the target was plainly visible.

By June 1968, the decision was made to disestablish VO-67, but the date was pushed back in deference to the Air Force's request that the Neptunes remain for an extended period until the 25th Tactical Fighter Squadron could assume the mission. After an additional month, VO-67 was notified that

An OP-2E from VO-67 in flight over the dense jungle of Thailand, en route to South Vietnam in an effort to monitor Communist movements. This aircraft was built as a P2V-5; changed to P-2E in 1962. (U.S. Navy)

it would be disestablished on July 1. The phaseout of operations and transfer of personnel began immediately, with all aircraft and men returning to the States by July 9. VO-67 was a unique, and uniquely short-lived, squadron. It was not followed by another similar unit and its activities have remained largely unchronicled. The men of the squadron overcame many unusual administrative and operational problems, including lack of formalized training and clerical help, weather and enemy defenses to accomplish their assigned mission.

Other special Navy aircraft fought their own anti-truck war, including the EAK-3B, yet another development of the venerable Skywarrior; the new A-6C TRIM previously described; and the backbone F-4 and A-4/A-7 combinations. Thousands of trucks were destroyed by Air Force and Navy aircraft, but the influx of supplies and men into the south hardly slowed. By not cutting the stream of supplies off at the source, in Hanoi, Haiphong, Cam Pha and other North Vietnamese population centers, the campaign against the Ho Chi Minh Trail convoys was doomed to failure from the start.

Another of the many unsung units of the Vietnam War was Heavy Photographic Squadron 61, operating twin-jet RA-3B Skywarriors in various detachments from Guam to Da Nang and Don Muang Airfield in Thailand. VAP-61's mission was primarily cartographic photography, the large A-3 providing a near-ideal platform for the exacting work of mapping photography, as well as in-flight access to the several cameras. Active from the beginning of hostilities, VAP-61 provided new cartographic imagery to update old French maps, dating back some twenty years.

However, after the November 1, 1968 bombing halt, the RA-3Bs were given an intelligence-gathering mission along the Ho Chi Minh Trail—first during the day, and then, after the loss of two aircraft to small-arms fire, at night. Outfitted with infrared sensors, as well as a video real-time display, the A-3s roamed up and down the trails looking for night truck traffic. Usually flying no higher than 500 feet, the RA-3B's crew would train their sensors, looking for "hot spots," indicating traffic on a road. Keeping track of the trucks on his video console, the crewman could call down orbiting A-4s from the offshore carriers to "pounce" on the traffic. Although the VAP-61 aircraft flew sometimes three missions a night, the best time seemed to be near dawn, when the Viet Cong drivers pulled their trucks off the trail to hide them during the day. These concentrations of vehicles created larger hot spots which showed up accordingly on the video console, indicating a larger target for the A-4s. Forty-man dets were established at Da Nang in January 1968, which permitted the aircraft to operate with more than one carrier group each night, increasing the aircraft's effectiveness.

Another facet of VAP-61 (and its sister unit, VAP-62, which operated under 61's authority at Da Nang), was its camouflage-detection activity, using a special infrared film. This CDIR film could detect whether or not vegetation was alive. The Communists were adept at camouflaging their truck parts with cut trees. The special film could show when dead trees covered over a suspected area. After five and one-half years of combat operation, VAP-61 was decommissioned in 1970.

THE INVASION OF LAOS

North Vietnamese buildups dating from late 1970 in the panhandle region of the Vietnams seemed to indicate a forthcoming invasion of Cambodia and/ or Laos and South Vietnam by early 1971. It was clear that American forces would be needed to counter this threat. Accordingly plans were drawn up, codenamed Lam Son 719, commemorating a Vietnamese victory over the Chinese in the fifteenth century. South Vietnamese units jumped off from Quang Tri province in northern South Vietnam and made their way to Tchepone just over the Laotian border on February 8, 1971. Under an umbrella of United States aircraft, South Vietnamese units actually crossed into Laos, enabling America to point to its program of Vietnamization of the war, and its own phased withdrawal of troops from the combat zone.

However, the North Vietnamese put up strong opposition and the South Vietnamese forces finally had to call for helicopter pickups in several areas, sometimes under heavy fire. By March 25 the last South Vietnamese had left Laos, with Hanoi and Saigon both claiming victory. Although the Saigon government claimed disruption of the supply routes, seemingly within a week, reconnaissance pilots reported traffic once again on the trails, moving towards the south.

The 27-Charlie-class carrier *Hancock* operated in support of Lam Son 719, along with other ships. The smaller, World War II-era ship included among its complement of aircraft, the veteran A-4 Skyhawk. The rugged little attack bomber had been somewhat eclipsed by the more sophisticated A-7 Corsair II, but the A-4 was very much in evidence on the smaller carriers like the *Hancock*. VA-55 and 164 made up the attack capability of Air Wing 21, operating A-4Fs, which included increased avionics in a humped fairing behind the cockpit.

The A-4s were largely responsible for anti-truck

attacks along the Ho Chi Minh Trail through Laos, as well as providing support for Marine ground operations in South Vietnam. There were also the occasional retaliatory raids into southern North Vietnam. Working in conjunction with Air Force Forward Air Controllers (FACs) in OV-10s, the *Hancock* A-4s operated mainly in the passes—Mu Gia, Ban Karai and Ban Raving—on the Laos-Vietnam border, sometimes going into the so-called Laotian Panhandle, which was actually Air Force territory nicknamed Steel Tiger.

Strikes were flown night and day against vehicular traffic, and results varied, as to how many trucks were hit and destroyed. Representative of the character of this operations is the November 21, 1970 mission flown by VA-55 A-4Fs during a mid-afternoon hop near Cape Mui Ron. With a 6,000-foot ceiling, the A-4s spotted trucks and made an unsuccessful attack, dropping some of their Mark 82 bombs. Several other runs proved inconclusive, the low ceiling making a textbook run-in difficult. Flak began to appear as well.

With their bombs gone, the A-4 pilots were thinking of going home, when a call came that another flight had some Communist trucks bottled up on a road nearby. The Skyhawks headed for the area and found the trucks, hitting several. Finally, calling "Winchester," which was the radio code for having used all ammunition, the VA-55 aviators headed for the *Hancock*.

Flak was the only constant opposition which the truck strikers faced, and the pilots took the nearby appearance of puffs of smoke in stride. However,

A "humped-back" A-4F Skyhawk from VA-22 on the *Bon Homme Richard* circles over the carrier in preparation for landing as the carrier steams through the Gulf of Tonkin. The A-4 series underwent a continued series of modifications after its original design by Ed Heinemann in the early 1950s as a daylight-only nuclear delivery aircraft. (U.S. Navy, W. E. Bradford)

occasionally the Communists moved larger guns into an area, especially those which could be radar-directed, like 57-mm weapons, and the A-4 drivers became instantly more alert to the danger.

The Skyhawks were also responsible for Iron Hand anti-SAM missions, where two aircraft were armed with beam-riding Shrike missiles which could be launched against any SAM site posing a threat to the larger strike force. Sometimes the hunters became the hunted, as on the mission of April 28, 1971. Four A-4s launched from *Hancock* to escort a photo plane towards a supposedly unoccupied SAM

259

site. Soon after coasting in, the lights in the cockpits of the A-4s started lighting up with SAM warnings. With the warble of a radar warning droning in their ears, the pilots saw a brilliant orange flash in the west, as a SAM rose towards them. With training instilled since the earliest days of flight indoctrination, the leader called for the flight to break right, hoping to give someone a chance to fire a Shrike at the incoming SAM. But the missile was too close, and seemed to have a good lock on the A-4s, as it matched their evasive maneuvers.

Then one of the pilots broke into the missile's flight path and executed a steep dive, which the missile could not immediately follow. Watching the SAM, the A-4 pilot pulled out of his dive and then into a hard left roll and steep climb. The missile, which by now was much too close to correct, failed to correct towards the desperate Skyhawk and passed some 800 feet below the flight. A second missile now approached the group—but similar action evaded this threat too, and the A-4s headed towards the SAM site, allowing the photo plane to get its coverage of the "unoccupied SAM site."

The A-4s were called in to aid most any kind of air-support task. During Lam Son 719, they supported ground operations as the South Vietnamese units tried to push the Viet Cong and North Vietnamese regulars out of Laos. In mid-February, a flight was called in near Khe Sanh, but as they approached the area they found a great deal of confusion between air-force units, other Navy flights, the FAC, and ground units calling for help.

As the FAC evidently called for some to jettison their ordnance, the pilots could hear an army helicopter crewman call for help on the emergency frequency. His helicopter had been shot down and he was rapidly being surrounded by Communist troops. Another chopper made it through ground fire, but could only pick up four of the first plane's crew, leaving the one man on the ground. As the pilots of other helicopters keyed their radios, the constant chatter of their gunner's machine guns could be heard in the background. In desperation the A-4 pilot called for some coordination from the FAC aircraft but got no response, and with their fuel low, they were forced to drop their bombs in a tree line, leaving the action on the ground. Tired and frustrated, the Skyhawk pilots recovered aboard the *Hancock*.

Many times, especially during this sort of "limbo" period for American carrier groups, the rationale of the war and its operation was questioned by many of the men who every day flew from the ships, putting their lives on the line. This is not to say that these men in any way did less of a job, but as intelligent and trained individuals, they naturally wondered about how such controlled confusion — sometimes uncontrolled — could possibly win the war. Lieutenant Eliot Tozer III, a VA-55 A-4 pilot, wrote in his diary:

The frustration comes on all levels. We fly a limited aircraft, drop limited ordnance, on rare targets in a severely limited amount of time. Worst of all, we do all this in a limited and

ASW carriers performed a variety of support roles in the Vietnam War while able to counter possible interference with naval operations by Soviet submarines. Here an SH-3A Sea King and a Marine A-4 Skyhawk stand ready on the deck of the *Hornet*. The Sea King prepares to fly a rescue mission and the Skyhawk "fighter"—armed with 20-mm cannon and Sidewinder missiles—to provide air patrol. (U.S. Navy)

An A-7A Corsair from VA-97 is about to be catapulted from the carrier *Constellation* to strike a target offshore. The black cross on the nose gave early indication to the landing signal officer (LSO) that the plane was an A-7 and not the similar-looking F-8 Crusader. The heavier A-7 required different arresting gear settings; the heavier EA-6B was similarly marked to distinguish it from the A-6. (U.S. Navy)

highly unpopular war. . . . the nature of our war on the tactical level cannot be even partially dispelled, however. Our ordnance load is limited to less than two tons of explosives . . . We're in, have time for two runs and we're bingo for either time or fuel.

All theories aside, what I've got is personal pushing against a tangled web of frustration. One of the ways to slice through the webbing and be free, at least for the moment, of almost all frustration is to press the attack home and while you jink and claw away from all the reaching AAA hear the FAC—"Shit-hot, two, you got the son of a bitch!"

Much of the problem came from the fact that targets were assigned by the Air Force, in coordination with Forward Air Controllers. If, when the A-4s arrived over their area, the FAC could find no targets or activity for them, the sorties were wasted, the bombs had to be jettisoned, and morale plunged accordingly.

The other units aboard the carriers, especially the usually glamorous fighter squadrons, were little more than hand-maidens to the attack squadrons, flying escort for photo missions, or waiting endless hours on deck in an alert status for the MiG threat which never came. Duty pilots were supposed to sit in the aircraft, strapped into their seats, engines turning, ready to scramble in a moment's notice. During these two- and three-hour stretches, their discomfort is hard to imagine if one has never sat in a fighter's ejection seat, with very little cushioning between one and the metal pan which contained necessary survival gear. Eventually some squadrons allowed their duty pilots to be in the ready rooms, in flight gear, ready to dash to the aircraft should the need arise.

Throughout the war, as with all fleet operations, the need to get material, replacement parts, supplies and mail to the carrier at sea was a constant operational consideration. Two aircraft which per-

An A-4F from VA-55 aboard the carrier *Hancock* releases a load of bombs over the Ho Chi Minh trail during the long and frustrating effort to interdict the overland supply routes from North Vietnam into the South. (Eliot Tozer)

A C-1A Trader COD aircraft about to touch down on a carrier. These slow-flying cargo and passenger planes, and the larger C-2A Greyhounds, kept up a flow of spare parts, mail, and passengers to and from the fleet at sea throughout the Vietnam War. (U.S. Navy)

formed this valuable service almost exclusively were the Grumman C-1 Trader and C-2 Greyhound, cargo versions of the S-2 Tracker ASW aircraft and E-2 Hawkeye AEW turboprop, respectively. VRC-50, the Pacific Fleet tactical support squadron, flew its detachment aircraft out to the carriers on combat duty in the South China Sea. The large C-2 could carry 1,600 pounds of mail to the waiting ships. Operating from NAS Cubi Point, Philippines, the Carrier On-board Delivery (COD) aircraft were a necessary part of daily operations which received little recognition.

9

Resumed Intensity

The failure of the Laotian anti-truck campaign to halt, or at least slow down, the flow of supplies to the south seemed to set the stage for a major action by the North Vietnamese. As the New Year rolled around, U.S. air activity was stepped up as protective-reaction raids below the 20th parallel occurred with increasing regularity. The Communists were known to be bringing increasing numbers of mobile SAM sites towards the DMZ. The threat was becoming more and more obvious; in the last three weeks of 1971, ten American aircraft were lost, from a variety of combat measures, over North Vietnam and Laos. In the first three months of 1972, ninety protective-reaction raids were flown by Navy and Air Force planes against the SAM and AAA installations, compared with 103 strikes during all of 1971.

Mk-82 500-pound bombs released by an A-4 Skyhawk of VA-55 from the *Hancock* fall on an enemy target in Vietnam. The bombs' folding fins have not yet opened. (Eliot Tozer)

Off the coast, only the *Coral Sea* and *Constellation* patrolled their beat, both ships on their sixth combat cruise. *Hancock* soon joined them in early February 1972. The carriers were under the command of Admiral John S. McCain II, now CINCPAC. His father had commanded TF 38 from the *Hancock* in the 1945 strikes against the Japanese in Indochina twenty-seven years before; and it was from *Hancock* that his son, Lieutenant Commander John S. McCain III, flew his last strike on October 26, 1967, when he was shot down and taken prisoner by the North Vietnamese.

Nineteen seventy-two was to become a pivotal year for the American forces in this long, frustrating war, especially in the air war. The battle between the MiGs and American fighters was rejoined on January 19, 1972, when an F-4J of VF-96 off *Constellation* shot down a MiG-21, the 112th MiG kill of the war, and the tenth MiG-21 brought down by the Navy. Spotting a section of MiG-21s during a photo escort mission, the F-4 crew flew right up behind the lead MiG and shot a Sidewinder missile at him at only 600 feet altitude. The missile missed, and the two MiGs began to run. In the twisting pursuit, the F-4 fired a second missile which found its mark and blew the entire tail section off the North Vietnamese fighter.

The elated pilot and his Radar Intercept Officer (RIO) flew back to the *Constellation*. These two men could not know it then, but they were to become the Navy's first and only aces of the Vietnam War, and the first recognized "team" aces in aerial warfare. Lieutenant Randy Cunningham and

Getting ready: an A-4F Skyhawk from VA-212 receives tender loving care from hangar deck personnel aboard the *Hancock*. Two drop tanks and a center-line in-flight refueling pod is fitted to this plane, to permit it to refuel other A-4s in flight.

Lieutenant (j.g.) Willie Driscoll had to wait four months for their second kill, however.

Meanwhile, a VF-111 F-4 crew made the next kill on March 28. Vectored towards a MiG during a photo-escort mission, two F-4Bs from *Coral Sea* engaged a MiG-17, but the tighter-turning North Vietnamese was able to get behind the lead American fighter. After a series of turns, the F-4 was able to regain his advantage and fire off a Sidewinder missile. The MiG-17 pilot wrapped his plane up into a tight turn, escaping the missile. The lead called for his wingman to try his luck, and the second F-4B pulled right behind the MiG and fired another Sidewinder. This one guided perfectly, and brought the MiG down.

It was not until May that Navy aircraft scored another kill, but this month was to be the most productive month for American carrier pilots in the entire war, with sixteen MiGs downed, as well as an unidentified aircraft which ventured too far out towards the cruiser *Chicago* in the gulf of Tonkin and was shot down by a Talos surface-to-air missile. VF-96, 51, 114, and 161 all scored MiG kills, with VF-96 leading the pack with seven. Four of those MiGs went to the team of Cunningham and Driscoll.

THE FIRST ACES

VF-96 had been one of the premier fighter squadrons during the war and for two straight years had been awarded the Clifton Trophy, given to the Navy's most outstanding fighter squadron. VF-96 sailed on the *Constellation* in October 1971, as part of CVW-9 to engage in the first large-scale bombing of the North since 1968. Arriving on Yankee Station, VF-96 was immediately engaged in strike and support missions in Laos, and South and North Vietnam. The ship and its air wing were extended due to the massive buildups in the North, and on May 8 Cunningham and Driscoll got their second kill, a MiG-17, as well as a truck which they shot with a remaining Sidewinder on the way back to the carrier.

It was during a classic Alpha strike two days later, that the VF-96 team was to earn themselves a place in the history books. On May 10, 1972, VF-96 was part of a large attack on the rail yards of Hai Duong, between Hanoi and Haiphong. The launch from *Constellation* went at 1130, and seven F-4Js from VF-96 accompanied the air wing, each Phantom with 2,000 pounds of ordnance for flak suppression.

The accompanying A-6s and A-7s went after the railway yards, while the F-4s engaged the estimated twenty-two MiGs which intercepted the strike force. Dodging SAMs and flak, the VF-96 F-4s dropped their bombs on a large storage building, and climbed back to engage the MiG force. Two MiG-17s got behind Cunningham and Driscoll's wingman, with Cunningham some 1,000 feet out in front. As Cunningham swung his F-4 around to meet the threat, the MiG made the mistake of exposing his underside to the F-4 for a split second in a vertical climb. Cunningham shot a Sidewinder up his tailpipe, and the MiG exploded. Turning back into the fight, Cunningham and Driscoll baited another MiG-17, pulling him across his wingman's line of fire. (Cunningham had promised a few days earlier to give his wingman a chance at a kill, if the opportunity arose.) But the other F-4 was occupied with other MiGs, and Cunningham used his aircraft's superior power to disengage from the MiG-17.

Looking around, they spotted a Phantom with two MiGs on his tail, and another off his right wing. Maneuvering behind the closest MiG, while

Outspoken and well-liked John S. McCain, Jr., served as Commander-in-Chief Pacific, directing all U.S. military operations in the vast theater, from July 1968 until September 1972. A submariner, he was the son of one of the Navy's most famous aviators. (U.S. Navy)

keeping his eye on the other enemy fighters, Cunningham fired another Sidewinder which blew the MiG-17 up, its pilot ejecting. Four MiG-21s which had been circling above, now joined the action, and the outnumbered F-4 crew pointed their airplane's nose for home. Heading for the coast, Cunningham spotted another MiG-17 down low, and with four kills, he went after his fifth.

There is some data which suggests that this MiG-17 was flown by a leading North Vietnamese ace credited with thirteen American kills, but as much of the information surrounding this man's identity and how it became known is classified, public confirmation is lacking. Cunningham and Driscoll engaged the camouflaged MiG-17 in a swirling dogfight with both aircraft trading advantages. Cunningham knew he had met a really good North Vietnamese pilot, whatever his true identity. Finally the MiG pilot disengaged and headed away, perhaps because he was low on fuel. He had placed himself at an ultimately fatal disadvantage. The F-4, now above and behind him, shot his last Sidewinder at the returning MiG. The missile guided perfectly and blew the enemy fighter apart.

With his missiles gone, and his fuel low, Cunningham now turned in earnest for the water. Coasting out near Haiphong, the F-4 was hit by a SAM, and after trying to nurse the crippled plane back to the *Constellation*, the two men ejected at 10,000 feet altitude. They were picked up by a helicopter and returned to their carrier where they were interviewed and feted as the first American aces of the Vietnam War.

"Lady Jessie," honoring a pilot's mother, became a tradition in VA-164 aboard the *Hancock*. An A-4 was given the name during each cruise, in this view with VA-164 flying the A-4F as the carrier's fourth squadron.

May 10, 1972, saw a total of seven MiGs destroyed by Navy pilots; three Navy Crosses were eventually awarded to men who flew during the day's intensive air strikes. One award went to the air wing commander, Commander Lowell F. Eggert, who planned and directed the strike from an A-7 of VA-146. The two remaining Navy Crosses were awarded to the crew of a VF-96 F-4J, Lieutenant Matthew J. Connelly III, the pilot, and his RIO, Lieutenant Thomas J. Blonski. Connelly and Blonski scored two MiG-17 kills while covering the raid over the rail yards, intercepting a force of five MiGs.

275

May continued to be a good month for the Navy pilots. May 18 saw two MiG-19s downed by two F-4s, and on the 23rd, a double MiG-17 kill was scored by a VF-161 F-4B from the *Midway*. Vectored to MiGs by the destroyer *Biddle*, two VF-161 F-4Bs found themselves directly over the large Kep MiG base. Two silver colored MiG-19s flew in front of the American fighters, and as the F-4s turned to pursue the MiGs, they found the sky was full of MiG-17s. A MiG tacked itself onto the lead F-4 and in his haste to reverse his position, the Navy pilot stalled his plane and began tumbling end-over-end. Finally righting the Phantom, he saw a MiG-17 pass right in front of him. He quickly squeezed off a missile, which tracked towards the MiG; but at the last instant, the MiG broke away and the missile missed.

Engaging another MiG-17, the frustrated F-4 crew was able to fire another Sidewinder as the MiG flew in front of them. This missile tracked perfectly and blew the MiG's tail off. With no time to catch their breath, the Phantom crew turned towards their wingman who had a MiG on his tail. Racing towards their comrade, the first F-4 pilot shot off another missile, and the MiG went down.

June was not as intense as May; only three MiGs were shot down, but the action was constant. Commander Sam Flynn, the Executive Officer of VF-31 off *Saratoga*, scored a MiG-21 kill on June 21. This was the first kill attained by aircraft from an Atlantic fleet carrier. The F-4 was on a MiG Combat Air Patrol (MiG CAP) when it engaged three MiG-21s over North Vietnam.

The winning team of Lieutenant Randall H. Cunningham, left, and Lieutenant (j.g.) William Driscoll relax aboard the carrier *Constellation* after being rescued from the waters just off the North Vietnamese coast. They were the nation's first aces of the war, having downed five MiGs while flying the F-4 Phantom. They were shot down by a SAM shortly after their fifth kill. (U.S. Navy)

Part of the success story was the radar controllmen on the ships of TF 77. Stationed off the North Vietnamese coast, these cruisers and destroyers, such as the *Chicago* and *Biddle*, focused their elaborate radar systems on MiG activity and warned American aircraft of any MiG presence, usually vectoring fighters towards the MiG threat. One man, Chief Radarman Larry H. Nowell, was officially cited for having participated in intercepts that resulted in the downing of twelve MiGs. Stationed in the missile cruiser *Chicago,* codenamed Red Crown, Chief Nowell was responsible for sev-

This photo of the *Constellation's* flight deck was taken on May 9, 1972, a day before Phantom crewmen Driscoll and Cunningham had a most successful day in the air war over North Vietnam. Parking aircraft on a flight deck is an art, in view of their size, varying mission requirements, the limited space, and the need to maintain, fuel, and arm the aircraft. (U.S. Navy, B.V. Little)

eral of the successful encounters during May 1972. The tenth, a great day for the Navy fighter crews, saw three of the downed MiGs credited to the Chief's directional efforts.

Another ship-based radar station was PIRAZ, Positive Identification Radar Advisory Zone. These ships provided information on everything from navigation to airborne threats for the aircraft of the Navy and Air Force. The Air Force had its own versions of PIRAZ and Red Crown vessels: College Eye, and the later Disco, EC-121 Constellations orbited Laos and the Gulf of Tonkin, assisting aircraft in finding or escaping MiG threats.

The increased MiG activity in 1972 also enabled the Air Force to gain its first aces, albeit three months after the Navy. Captain Steve Ritchie downed his fifth MiG on August 28; his back-seater, Captain Charles DeBellevue gained his fifth kill on September 9, 1972, as well as a sixth kill during the same flight. These double kills made DeBellevue the leading American ace of the conflict. The Air Force's third ace of the Vietnam War was Captain Jeffrey Feinstein, and like DeBellevue was a navigator weapons system officer (WSO). Feinstein got his fifth MiG on October 13.

The Marines were also finally able to chalk up their first kill, with an all-Marine crew flying a Marine aircraft. Marine planes had been flying from Navy carriers since 1971, the first time Marine tactical units had flown from Navy ships since the early 1960s. VMA(AW)-224 had been the first Marine A-6 squadron to fly combat missions from Navy carriers. They flew interdiction missions from the *Coral Sea*, supported South Vietnamese troop operations and also participated in aerial mining operations. The *America* included VMFA-333 as one of its air wing's fighter squadrons, and it was a Phantom of 333 which scored a kiss on September 11, 1972. Major Lee Lasseter, the Executive Officer of the squadron, and his RIO, Captain John Cummings, together with their wingman, engaged two MiG-21s three miles north of Hanoi. Lasseter and Cummings quickly destroyed one of the MiGs, and the second North Vietnamese fighter retreated away from the fight. However, this MiG returned as the Marine jets headed back towards their carrier. The MiG-21 made a run on Lasseter's wingman but was driven off with another Sidewinder from Lasseter which apparently inflicted some damage on the MiG.

Heading towards the coast, Lasseter's and Cumming's aircraft was hit by a SAM. Their wingman's F-4 was also damaged, apparently in one of the fuel cells; both crews finally ejected south of Haiphong, where they were picked up by SAR helicopter. Despite the loss of the Phantoms, the Marines had finally been able to score a MiG kill on their own. Major Lasseter was awarded the Alfred E. Cunningham Award as the top Marine aviator in 1972. He had scored the first all-Marine kill since World War II. (Marines had gained several MiGs in Korea, but always while on exchange duty with the Air Force.) He also assumed command of VMFA-333 on December 24, when Lieutenant Colonel J.K. Cochran and his RIO were shot down by antiaircraft fire during a photo escort mission on December 23.

The intense air-to-air combat of 1972 gave a good indication of the value of such training programs as Top Gun. Several of the kills gained during this period were scored by Top Gun graduates. Admiral Elmo Zumwalt, Chief of Naval Operations, noted that the current ratio of 12-to-1 was a "tremendous testimony to the training, skill and courage of our combat aircrews . . ." Students who attended the Fighter Weapons School prior to deploying to Vietnam were enthusiastic in their praise of the curriculum, once they had engaged in actual aerial combat, saying "It was just like the hassles at Top Gun!"

EASTER INVASION

The main reason for the increase in air activity was the buildup in material by North Vietnam and the subsequent invasion of the South on March 30. On that Thursday before Good Friday, three North Vietnamese divisions pushed through the DMZ. Eventually over 120,000 troops, twelve of Hanoi's thirteen regular combat divisions, were sent into South Vietnam during the Easter weekend. The border town of An Loc was besieged, as the South's troops fell back against the Communist onslaught; the North was using tanks in force for the first time in the war. One North Vietnamese division headed towards Hue, rolling over former American bases at Khe Sanh, Con Thien, and Camp Carroll in Quang Tri province. SAMs and hundreds of Soviet T-54, T-

A4-Es of VMA-311 in their revetments at Da Nang, June 1972. The "Tomcats" had returned to South Vietnam to counter the Easter Invasion. (USMC)

34, and PT-76 tanks faced the South's defenders, primarily green, untried troops.

The Arc Light operation, B-52 strikes, was almost immediately expanded as the bombers were called in from Guam. The Stratofortresses struck the enemy troop concentrations at An Loc from April through May, giving the South Vietnamese forces breathing space and time to re-group to counter the Communist invasion. May 1 saw a reorganized defense of Hue begin, with reinforced southern divisions finally wresting control of the besieged area from the Communists. The South had made good use of antitank weapons, slowing the advance of the north's armored forces, while the B-52 raids and Navy offshore fire support held the North Vietnamese down.

The invasion galvanized America's military into action. Besides ordering step-ups in B-52 operations, an order for the Marines to return to Vietnam sent several squadrons of aircraft scrambling back from their bases in Japan and the United States. There had only been about 500 Marines in Vietnam by mid-1971, but less than a year later the situation had changed completely. On April 5, two F-4 squadrons, VMFA-115 and 232, were ordered to return, which the units did the next day, landing at Da Nang as part of Marine Air Group 15. Commencing combat operations on April 9, the squadrons were joined by VMFA-212, which had flown in from Hawaii, as well as the carrier-based A-6s of VMA(AW)-224 from the *Coral Sea*.

In addition, the A-4 returned to South Vietnam, when VMA-211 and 311 flew into the base at Bien

Hoa, which was a new base for the Marines. Operations from Bien Hoa began on May 19, with the main effort concentrating along the Cambodian and Laotian border invasion points.

The Marine effort was expanded into northern Thailand, when the F-4J squadrons, VMFA-115 and VMFA-232, were sent to the partially completed field at Nam Phong, 300 miles from Da Nang, and about the same distance from Hanoi. Begun five years earlier as a support facility, Nam Phong had never been finished. Navy Construction Battalions were sent in, the 10,000-foot runway was completed, and the F-4 squadrons, along with A-6s of VMA(AW)-533, began operation on June 24. The Marines who lived and flew from Nam Phong called the austere facility the "Rose Garden."

The Easter invasion had caught the Navy undermanned in the Gulf of Tonkin. Only the carriers *Coral Sea* and *Hancock* were on station; *Constellation* had made a side trip to Hong Kong, and was immediately recalled. *Kitty Hawk* soon joined the task force, while *Enterprise* was on duty in the Indian Ocean. The nuclear carrier had been dispatched at the outbreak of the Indo-Pakistani War and was the flagship for TF 74, which was intended to show the flag in the South Asian area during the hostilities. By July, six carriers were on the line, the greatest number of the war, as well as other ships in the process of transiting the Pacific.

Nineteen seventy-two had been designated as the Year of the Carrier, in commemoration of the 50th anniversary of the commissioning of the Navy's first "flattop," the USS *Langley* (CV-1). Along with the commemorative observances, a new concept in carrier operations was being initiated: the CV. Carriers had been designated CVAs, for Attack Carrier, while some had been designated CVS, for Antisubmarine Carrier. The retirement of the ASW carriers, however, and the development of the specialized jet ASW aircraft, the Lockheed S-3, gave rise to the new overall concept of one ship carrying out all phases of the two different operations, supposedly giving greater flexibility to Navy operations and mission planning. The first ship to be designated as a CV was the *Saratoga*, an Atlantic Fleet carrier which was hurriedly recalled from the other side of the country to augment the force off Vietnam in April 1972. She carried, in addition to normal attack aircraft, Sea King helicopters as part of her new ASW capability.

The fast-paced events of the Easter invasion thrust the *Saratoga* into combat operations. While most of her crew was ashore, the ship was quickly ordered to prepare for departure to the Pacific and South Vietnam. While a large-scale recall was initiated to get the crew back, a massive supply effort was begun by April 8. Within 60 hours, the big carrier was under way, after picking up her air wing, CVW-3. So sudden was the ship's departure from Mayport, Florida, that many of the crew's cars were left parked haphazardly on the pier, awaiting families to retrieve them. Although she had participated in various crisis deployments— Lebanon, 1957; the 1962 Cuban missile crisis; and several Mideast flare-ups—this was her first actual combat deployment.

After a month's transit to the Philippines for replenishment, the *Saratoga* arrived on Yankee Station on June 2, remaining on the line until June 21, the day when VF-31's executive officer, Commander Sam Flynn and his RIO, Lieutenant Bill John, scored the ship's first MiG kill. A second MiG was destroyed in the early evening of August 10, 1972, when the sister fighter squadron aboard, VF-103, shot down a second MiG-21 with two Sparrow missiles. Lieutenant Commander Gene Tucker and Lieutenant (j.g.) Bruce Edens, Jr., received credit for the kill, which was the first score at night for a Navy fighter with a Sparrow.

The *Saratoga's* aircraft flew hundreds of missions supporting South Vietnamese troops, hitting gun and mortar sites, bunkers, and supply areas near An Loc, where the Communists posed the strongest threat, as well as strikes in the Mekong Delta and near Saigon. The planes of CVW-3 also ranged farther north, to Haiphong, hitting railway yards and bridges around the port city. The fighters, besides escorting the large A-6 and A-7 bomber forces, also contributed to the strike effort with the use of so-called "smart bombs" (laser-guided weapons), and conventional iron bombs.

Saratoga was obviously not alone in the Gulf during the furious action of April–May 1972. *Hancock, Midway, Constellation,* and *Kitty Hawk* all sent their air wings against the North Vietnamese offensive. The advantage of the carrier as a roving airfield, able to go where and when needed, was proved time and again as the ships patrolled the entire length of Vietnam, their planes striking at

An E-2B Hawkeye from Airborne Early Warning Squadron (VAW) 116 is launched from the *Constellation* during the hectic April 1972 carrier operations off Vietnam. While fighter and attack aircraft's exploits took most of the headlines, on a day-to-day basis the AEW aircraft, tankers, COD, and, of course, the reconnaissance planes carried a large burden of the war effort. (U.S. Navy, Ronald F. Reichwein)

enemy positions in Quang Tri, South Vietnam one day, and then hitting targets in Haiphong the next. The veteran *Hancock,* still using the equally venerable A-4 Skyhawk, concentrated on truck and troop positions in the south. The larger ships, *Constellation* and *Kitty Hawk,* carried the more sophisticated A-7 and A-6, using them against antiaircraft artillery sites, as well as bunkers and supply depots.

In the midst of the fighting, *Hancock* passed her twenty-eighth birthday. *Midway,* which was almost of the same vintage as *Hancock,* and her air wing,

CVW-5, also participated in the intensive strikes, her aircraft racking up several MiG kills during the hectic month of May.

THE MINING OPERATION – AT LAST

Even in the midst of the all-out invasion, the United States tried to show some restraint. Indeed, for over two years the President's National Security Advisor, Dr. Henry Kissinger, had been holding secret and public meetings with the North Vietnamese representative, Le Duc Tho, in Paris, trying to arrive at a ceasefire agreement. The North Vietnamese played for time, alternatively agreeing, then disagreeing, with the American representatives.

Finally, on May 2, Kissinger confronted Tho five days after the North had unleashed what Kissinger called "the heaviest artillery barrage of the war and large numbers of tanks." In a frustrating exchange, the wily Tho tried to intimidate Kissinger with wide-ranging references to American unrest at home and dissatisfaction with the war, intimating that the North Vietnamese now held the upper hand and were convinced of their ultimate victory in the South. There was little for Kissinger to do but report back to President Nixon that, once more, the Vietnamese had proved intransigent.

In what Kissinger referred to as "one of the finest hours of Nixon's presidency," the President, for the first time in the war, ordered the mining of Haiphong and other important harbors of North Vietnam to curb the flow of supplies. With a strategic summit meeting between Nixon and Soviet President Brezhnev in the final planning stages, the strong possibility of intensified public outcry at home, and the imminent collapse of South Vietnam facing him, Nixon had decided to gamble and shut off the flow of Soviet supplies at the source, rather than concentrate on battlefield actions. Kissinger wrote, "In an election year, he [Nixon] risked his political future on a course most of his Cabinet colleagues questioned."

The Navy had had a plan for the mining operation ready for some time. On May 8, squadrons of A-6s from three carriers sowed mine fields in Haiphong, Hon Gai, and Cam Pha in the north, and Thanh Hoa, Vinh, Quang Khe, and Dong Hoi in the south. The crews encountered heavy antiaircraft fire and SAMs, but the mines were dropped and by May 22, the *New York Times* reported that the mining operation had closed North Vietnam's ports; many merchant ships which were en route to North Vietnam were diverted elsewhere. Twenty-seven ships were caught in Haiphong Harbor and remained there, as the North Vietnamese made no attempt to clear the harbor of the mines. Vice Admiral William P. Mack, then Commander of the Seventh Fleet, was to write years later, "What happened was that all traffic into Vietnam, except across the Chinese border, stopped. Within ten days there was not a missile or a shell being fired at us from the beach. The North Vietnamese ran out of ammunition, just as we always said they would."

The American aerial offensive was given the code name Linebacker. Originally, the initial strikes had been called Freedom Train; the new name was given to include the mining operation. Along with the mining, the bombing strikes against the North were escalated to the most intense level of the war. The earlier Rolling Thunder operation of the first three years of the war was nothing compared to the impact of Linebacker in the first four months of the resumed strikes in 1972. In addition to the outright stopping of supplies to the south, the American strikes also were responsible for the failure of the North Vietnamese ground forces to take and hold areas. As the South Vietnamese regrouped and reengaged the enemy, under heavy U.S. air cover, the Communists fell back from Kontum, Pleiku, An Loc, and Quang Tri. Their plans for conquest had been thwarted because of the strangling of their supply lines, a step that American military commanders had maintained from the outset would bring about a North Vietnamese surrender, or at least make them more amenable at the peace conference table. Indeed, under the constant attack from carrier-based aircraft and Air Force fighter-bombers and giant B-52s, the Hanoi government began to show signs of an increased willingness to proceed more directly with the peace talks.

The B-52s had made their first raid over Hanoi and Haiphong on April 17. This raid stirred a storm of controversy about major escalation of the war by the United States, but the B-52s continued their strikes at the North Vietnamese capital until October 23, when it seemed that the Communists were about to ask for a ceasefire.

In the meantime, the six American carriers on

station in July—*America, Hancock, Kitty Hawk, Midway, Oriskany,* and *Saratoga*—continued sending waves of planes over the North and over contested areas in South Vietnam. A four-ship task unit was moved into position off Haiphong to shell the port city in August, while pilots from the *Midway* attacked PT-boat installations in the harbor. The aircraft of CVW-11 aboard the *Kitty Hawk* used a new version of the Walleye guided bomb, dubbed Fat Albert. This new modification could be used at a higher altitude than previous models, thus keeping the aircrews out of the range of enemy ground fire. *Oriskany* was on her seventh combat cruise of the war, and like the other carriers' planes, her aircraft ranged up and down Vietnam, hitting troop concentrations in South Vietnam as well as radar sites and supply barges in the North. The RF-8Gs of VFP-63's Det 4 flew reconnaissance missions over Haiphong and other anchorages, to keep track of the effect the mining operation was having on merchant traffic. The ship's aircraft performed the primary function of interdiction against the numerous supply trails, however, coordinating their strikes with Air Force Forward Air Controllers (FACs), much as they had been doing throughout the war.

Weather proved to be the greatest operational problem, especially when the plans called for flights up north. Clouds, fog, and rain seemed to hang off the northern coast, making the required bombing of specific targets sometimes impossible. In the south, even if the weather did not cooperate, strikes could still be conducted, using the TACAN-bombing method whereby the A-7s could release their bombs on an appropriate radar fix. But without the necessary ground installations up north, the weather was a much more serious factor.

Oriskany herself did not have an easy time of it during her last combat cruise. A faulty screw swung the carrier into the ammunition ship *Nitro,* during a night replenishment, resulting in the loss of one of *Oriskany's* aircraft elevators. The ship continued operations, however. But during this same line period, the ship *lost* a screw and had to retire to Yokosuka in Japan for major repairs. This period in drydock was the only liberty the ship's crew had during the line period, except for quick resupply detours to the Philippines.

THE FINAL RAIDS

The hope of October 1972 that the peace talks in Paris would soon produce a ceasefire quickly evaporated. For, after President Nixon had halted bombing attacks north of the 20th parallel, the Communists refused to deal in earnest, once the bombs stopped falling, and instead began using the respite to rebuild bombed areas and resupply their defenses. To rub salt in the wound, the North Vietnamese delegation walked out of the talks on December 13. Even America's erstwhile South Vietnamese allies seemed to turn against her, as South Vietnamese President Thieu, furious at Nixon for having reached what Thieu considered a separate peace with the North, plagued Kissinger and his team with sixty-nine major changes in the initial draft of the treaty.

With very little choice left to him, Nixon faced the decision which had plagued his predecessor, and which had stalked him since his inauguration: a maximum bombing effort, specifically aimed at the Hanoi-Haiphong complex. December 18 saw the first strikes of Linebacker II, as waves of B-52s and two-seater F-111s struck Hanoi and outlying airfields and complexes. A steel curtain of flak, SAMs, and MiGs met the attackers; three of the giant bombers were shot down. The tail-gunner of a B-52 claimed the first MiG kill by a B-52 when Staff Sergeant Samuel O. Turner, aboard a B-52D, shot down a MiG-21 as it tried to intercept the bomber force. A second MiG was destroyed by another B-52 gunner on December 24.

As the bombers pounded Hanoi, the American decision to unleash its strategic might met with some angry words in the press. *Time* magazine, which had recently selected both Nixon and Kissinger as its Men of the Year, maintained that "Nixon seemed determined to bomb Hanoi into a settlement that he is willing to accept." Radio Hanoi broadcast that American bombs had fallen in a POW camp, and that several prisoners had been wounded. Similarly, there was also apathy towards the bombing offensive, especially in the Congress. Confounded by the long years of endless conflict, the Senate and House were of a mind to cut funds for the war, and just turn it off, stop the war; the B-52 raids could be of little consequence.

Hanoi published magazine articles on the raids. "December 18, 1972. The American imperialists picked that beautiful moonlit night for their criminal undertaking against our capital city . . . Other raids, more barbarous, followed on subsequent nights." Other accounts featured North Vietnamese fighter pilots' stories of their battles with the B-52s and accompanying aircraft. Pham Tuan, a MiG-21 pilot, was credited with shooting down a B-52 during the December period, a claim the Americans strongly denied. Nguyen Duc Soat, another MiG-21 pilot, was credited with shooting down five American planes, including four F-4s during the period of May–October 1972. (One MiG-21 was credited with shooting down fourteen U.S. aircraft.)

Originally, the strikes of Linebacker had been flown by Thailand-based aircraft, but beginning with the attacks on May 21, B-52s from Guam also made the run. The Linebacker II attacks continued through December 24, Christmas Eve, with a 36-hour standdown over the holiday. On December 26, an elaborately planned strike hit Hanoi and Haiphong in a one-two-three stream of punches which proved to be the high point of the entire eleven-day Linebacker II Operation. Within a fifteen-minute period, over 100 B-52s struck the cities from three different directions, overtaxing and confusing the North Vietnamese defenses. Only two bombers were downed, one by a SAM over Hanoi, and the second made it back to Utapao, Thailand, but was destroyed during the landing. The Navy, prior to the actual arrival of the B-52s, sent in airfield suppression strikes, especially against Kep, the main MiG base in the Hanoi region, as well as other coastal airfields. These strikes were an effort to pin down the MiGs before the Air Force bombers arrived.

EW PROGRESS

During the heavy B-52 strikes in December, Navy and Marine EA-6As and EA-6Bs were indispensable in suppressing enemy defenses, just as they had been throughout the summer of 1972. One of the many unsung groups of the war, these squadrons of specially equipped A-6s with specially trained crews flew from carriers and land bases. The EA-6A was a modification of the original two-seat Intruder, equipped with tactical Electronic Counter Measures (ECM); it was delivered to the Marine Corps beginning in 1965 to replace the aging EF-10B Skyknight. VMCJ-1 became the first Marine A-6 squadron in Vietnam when the first EA-6As arrived in Da Nang that same year.

Experience with the two-seater gave rise to a requirement for an expanded capability and major modification designated EA-6B Prowler, which flew for the first time in 1968. After a long conversion period, the first Prowler deployment took place when VAQ-132 took its four aircraft aboard the *America* in June 1972. VAQ-131 sailed on the *Enterprise* later in September. The Prowler's main external modification was the lengthening of the fuselage by 40 inches to accommodate two additional crew members, bringing the total to four crewmen in each aircraft. A large fairing pod was also added to the vertical tail to hold several ECM

A prototype EA-6A Intruder electronic warfare aircraft being catapulted from a *Forrestal*-class carrier is loaded with four electronic jamming pods plus three drop tanks. The Marine Corps took delivery of all twenty-one EA-6A variants of the Intruder, with the Navy flying only the more capable EA-6B model. (U.S. Navy)

antennas which picked up signals from enemy radar and radio transmissions. These signals were then fed into an on-board computer and, within seconds, one of the four large active ECM pods hanging from wing stations would throw out massive energy beams to blind the enemy facilities, thereby protecting the strike force.

As with any large, expensive piece of military hardware, there were some initial bugs to be worked out. The EA-6B, which averaged about $26 million apiece, usually flew with only three crewmen, instead of the four accommodated. The man in the left rear seat was responsible for communications jamming, but since listening in on North Vietnam-

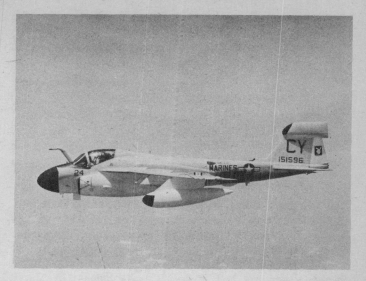

An EA-6A Intruder in flight with the markings of Marine Composite Reconnaissance Squadron (VMCJ) 2. At the time VMCJ squadrons operated both electronic jamming and photo reconnaissance aircraft of the Marine aircraft wings. The squadron's tail insignia was the Playboy bunny symbol. (U.S. Marine Corps)

ese radio transmissions was a major source of intelligence, there seemed little need for jamming in this area.

Another problem area was the coordination between the right front and the right rear Naval Flight Officers (there was only one pilot), who split radar jamming duties between them. These two men were responsible for jamming the target acquisition radars of SAM sites, as well as interceptor radar facilities, and during hectic action, the need to communicate with a second position could waste precious seconds.

This is a Navy EA-6B Prowler from VAQ-129, in flight with five jamming pods mounted. Each of the AN/ALQ-99 pods has two transmitters for jamming enemy radars, making the EA-6B the most capable aircraft of its type in operational service. The Navy changed the EA-6B's popular name from Intruder to Prowler in February 1972. (Grumman)

During the intense B-52 strikes in 1972, the electronic EA-6As and EA-6Bs were especially active, most crews flying three and even four hops a day to cover the incoming bomber forces. The Marines of VMCJ-1 operated from Cubi in the Philippines, using their own KC-130 tankers from VMGR-152 to extend their on-station time. Da Nang was used as a maintenance and secondary staging field. Such was the effort and the pace of the Marine operation, that it was not uncommon for *seven* EA-6As to be airborne at the same time, covering various strikes, especially during the December offensive. The Marines were particularly effective during this time frame because the North Vietnamese had apparently changed the guidance radar for their SA-2 Guideline SAMs. The new radar was in the high frequency I-Band range, and only the Marine EA-6As had the capability to jam this particular radar.

Navy EA-6Bs positioned themselves off the coast during the Arc Light strikes—they were prohibited from flying overland—to mask North Vietnamese SAM and antiaircraft fire-control radars aimed at the B-52s. The Prowlers were, however, mainly responsible for suppressing the Fansong target acquisition radar for the SA-2, which generated a broader beam and thus was easier to keep track of and suppress than other signals. Several SAMs were known to have exploded or missed their targets after having come under the attention of a patrolling Prowler.

The B-52 raids continued until December 29; the North Vietnamese had indicated a wish to return seriously to the bargaining table in Paris, and accordingly, President Nixon stopped the bombings. With the culmination of Linebacker II, aerial operations in Vietnam declined rapidly in intensity, waiting for the outcome of the peace talks. There had been only one MiG kill by Navy aircraft in December, the only one since the Marine score in September. An *Enterprise*-based F-4J of VF-142 shot down a MiG-21 on December 28. Aside from the two B-52-credited MiG kills in December during Linebacker II, the Air Force claimed three MiGs in December, all scored by F-4s.

So, as the ships of TF 77 steamed off the coast, and the Air Force waited at its bases in Guam and Thailand, the peace talks were set to resume on January 8, 1973. The atmosphere was cautiously hopeful. Linebacker II had been a tremendous effort. Nearly 1,000 SAMs had been thrown at the strike forces; nearly 3,500 sorties had been flown by B-52s, other tactical aircraft, and support aircraft. Fifteen B-52s had been shot down. But the entire Linebacker Operation, the mining, the intensive strikes at Hanoi and Haiphong, and reverses on the ground had finally brought the North Vietnamese around, at least for the moment. Admiral Thomas H. Moorer, then Chairman of the Joint Chiefs of Staff, said, "I am convinced that Linebacker II served as a catalyst for the negotiations."

10

A Doubtful Ending

The intense strikes of Linebacker II in December 1972, had evidently served their purpose when the North Vietnamese returned to the peace talks in Paris on January 6, 1973. Le Duc Tho, the chief negotiator for the Communists, had brought, it was hoped, an increased willingness to proceed as quickly and as meaningfully as possible towards a ceasefire. President Nixon had defeated his Democratic rival in the recent elections largely on his claim that he could and would end the war and bring the POWs home. The American public, having given him a mandate, demanded quick results. Tho was evidently under the same pressure from his government. The talks resumed while United States aircraft flew bombing strikes below the 20th parallel, beginning on January 3.

The Defense Department, on January 9, issued permission for fighters to pursue any MiGs which attacked the bombers, right up through the North Vietnamese panhandle, if necessary. It was soon afterwards that the last MiG kill was scored by an American aircraft. Lieutenant Victor Kovaleski and his RIO, Lieutenant Jim Wise, of VF-161 off the *Midway*, were vectored toward a MiG-17 over the northern part of the Gulf of Tonkin on January 12, and shot it down with two Sidewinders. Fighters from the *Midway* had shot down the first and last MiGs of the Vietnam War; on this cruise, VF-161's tally was five North Vietnamese MiGs. (In an odd twist, Lieutenant Kovaleski was also the pilot of the last aircraft to be shot down over the North, two days later, when he and his RIO, Ensign Dennis Plautz, were hit by antiaircraft fire on January 14. Ejecting from their Phantom, the two were picked up by helicopter in the Gulf and returned to the *Midway*.)

AIR-TO-AIR COMBAT

The Navy had accounted for 59 MiGs confirmed in air-to-air combat, as well as two AN-2 biplane transports, one probable MiG downed by a Talos SAM, and several probables. The Air Force could claim an official total of 137 MiGs shot down, including two by B-52 gunners, the final Air Force kill being registered by an F-4D over a MiG-21 on January 8, 1973.

The period of air-to-air combat provided by the Vietnam War had paradoxically proven both the validity and drawbacks of the all-missile-armed fighter, first proposed in the mid-1950s, and exemplified by the F-4. Although most of the Navy's kills were obtained solely with Sidewinder and Sparrow missiles, several were not. Some, at least, were scored with a combination of missiles and guns; the Air Force's total shows at least 30 percent by guns. While the missile was preferable at a distance, or at night, it was shown quickly that there was nothing a fighter pilot wanted more than an internally mounted gun, something he could depend on after his missiles were used, either by choice, or by the malfunction which was all too prevalent under the stresses of high-speed jet combat. After he had expended his Sidewinders and Sparrows, the only thing the Navy Phantom pilot had for defense was his mount's terrific speed, which was more often than not enough to get him and his RIO out of danger. But if he had sustained damage, was low on fuel, or was boxed in by tighter-turning MiGs, he was in trouble.

The Air Force realized the situation and installed a nose-mounted 20-mm cannon in their F-4E. But the Navy stuck to its missiles throughout the war, its primary fighter never enjoying the luxury of additional armament. The F-8 Crusader used both cannon and missile armament, although only one of the F-8's eighteen confimed MiG kills was obtained solely by gunfire. The Crusader's four 20-mm cannon posed problems early in the war, both the firing time and jamming. The first problem was eased somewhat by the provision of cockpit switches which allowed only two of the four cannons to be fired, thereby conserving ammunition.

The jamming problem was never fully eradicated.

The tactics of the Vietnam War were developed for high-speed combat. The "fluid-four" formation, harking back to the Thach Weave of World War II, was used for optimum visual and radar contact, should MiGs appear. Two flights of fighters would fly one above the other, the second flight weaving above and behind the lead flight with one aircraft in each flight responsible for visual search, one for radar search. Barrel Roll and Vertical Scissors attacks, trading speed for position, were used quite effectively against the MiG force which almost always enjoyed greater maneuverability, especially against the heavier F-4.

But the most important lesson learned during the period of aerial combat in Vietnam was the need for the gun. The impact of this discovery can be seen in every nation's fighter aircraft developed since the Vietnam War—American, British, French, Swedish, Israeli, and Russian. Every one has an integral 20- or 30-mm cannon.

THE CEASEFIRE

Finally, on January 23, 1973, a ceasefire was announced; the United States and North Vietnam had agreed on ending the fighting, returning the POWs, and clearing the harbors of mines. The newspapers carried the administration's declaration of "peace with honor." Aircraft from the *Enterprise* flew the last strikes in South Vietnam. On January 27, Commander Dennis Weichman, the CO of VA-

153, brought his Corsair back to *Oriskany* on the same day. As he rolled out of the arresting gear, Weichman was completing his final combat mission of the war, his 625th, the greatest number of any naval aviator.

The mining of North Vietnamese harbors in May 1972 had obviously called for a plan for clearing the mined areas, once ceasefire terms had been negotiated and signed. Accordingly, on November 1, the initial staff of Task Force 78 was established at Charleston, South Carolina. That same day, Helicopter Mine Countermeasures Squadron 12 (HM-12), which had been commissioned on April 1, 1971 and based at Norfolk, Virginia, began loading its CH-53A helicopters and support equipment aboard Air Force C-5A transports for deployment to the western Pacific. Provision was also made for the use of Marine helicopters to augment the Navy's capability. Sea Stallions of HMH-463, stationed in Hawaii, joined the Navy teams arriving in the Philippines. This was to be the first time that United States naval aircraft would conduct aerial minesweeping in a live minefield.

On January 27, 1973, four ocean minesweepers left Subic Bay in the Philippines for Haiphong, to begin Operation Endsweep, while modifications were being made to the Marine helicopters. The Marine aircraft had to be equipped to operate the 23-foot long magnetic hydrofoil sled which was towed from the CH-53, as well as other minesweeping devices. Other Marine units, HMM-164 and 165 practiced SAR techniques for the operation.

By February 24, the air units were ready to

A Marine CH-53A "on loan" to Navy Mine Countermeasures Squadron (HM) 12 skims over Haiphong harbor towing a hydrofoil minesweeping sled during Operation End Sweep. Note the large limestone formations that dotted the area. After End Sweep, HM-12 took delivery of specially designed RH-53D variants of the Sea Stallion. (U.S. Navy)

commence sweeping North Vietnamese harbors, the first mission being flown on the 27th by an HM-12 Sea Stallion in the main shipping channel of Haiphong. Occasionally halted because of political snags, Endsweep operations involved sunup-to-sundown flight operations, as well as nighttime maintenance and mission evaluation.

There were also delicate negotiations to be carried out with North Vietnamese personnel regarding their participation in the operation, and a training facility to acquaint the North Vietnamese with the various aspects of minesweeping operations was set up at Cat Bi airfield in Haiphong on March 26. By July 27, Operation Endsweep was concluded and Task Force 78 was disbanded, the mines having been cleared from North Vietnamese waters.

Marine Air Group 12, the last American combat aviation unit still in the country, had already left Vietnam, just as TF 78 had begun minesweeping. The first POWs to be released from North Vietnam arrived in the Philippines on February 12, and by March 29, 566 men had been returned.

It had been a very, very long war. Two thousand American airmen had been lost, with almost 1,400 fliers missing in action. Three thousand seven hundred American aircraft of all types had been destroyed in enemy action. A grand total of 7.4 million tons of bombs had been dropped throughout Indochina since 1965. But America's longest, most costly and frustrating war had come to an end. The POWs were home; American forces had disengaged and returned to their bases in the States and Japan—or had they? Americans would no longer fight and die in Southeast Asia—or would they? And, the South Vietnamese had been saved from the Communists in the North—hadn't they?

THE FALL OF SOUTH VIETNAM

The signing of a ceasefire agreement on January 23, 1973, did not mean the end of combat in

With war's end American fliers came back from captivity and deprivation in North Vietnam. The second POW in line is Navy Lieutenant Commander Fred R. Purrington; the others are Air Force fliers, waiting at Gia Lam airfield near Hanoi to board a plane for freedom on February 18, 1973.

Southeast Asia. Cambodia and Laos continued to fight against Communist insurgents which had been operating in these countries as long as their compatriots in Vietnam. As American withdrawals from Vietnam continued and the POWs returned home, Air Force and Navy aircraft flew strike missions into Laos. In Cambodia, the situation was desperate.

The capital of Phnom Penh, encircled by Communist forces, was virtually cut off from the world, and faced imminent starvation. Its only lifeline to the outside world was the convoys of ships which ran the Communist gauntlet along the Mekong River. Although supported by American aircraft, these ships suffered greatly from the Communists hidden along the banks. The convoy of April 5 barely made Phnom Penh with only eight of the original eighteen ships it started out with. Aircraft from *Enterprise*, as well as planes from Air Force units stationed in Thailand, conducted strikes against the enemy. The Communists protested over the American strikes as a major violation of the Paris accord. In response, the United States halted Project Endsweep operations, the clearing of mines from North Vietnam's harbors on April 19.

However, by June all sides had agreed to improve ceasefire enforcement, and by August 15 all American strikes against Cambodia and Laos were halted. The Laotians had accepted a coalition government, and the Cambodians were essentially left to fend for themselves. It was obvious that "peace with honor" had not been achieved by Dr. Kissinger, and that, in effect, the United States had been hoodwinked. The only positive result of the Paris talks had been the release of the POWs.

Although 566 POWs had returned home, there were many men still unaccounted for. Some were carried as Missing in Action, while others were listed as having been taken prisoner and not returned. While it was true that American ground forces had withdrawn by mid-1973, American servicemen were still flying support missions in Laos and Cambodia, dropping thousands of tons of ordnance on North Vietnamese-supported guerrillas, until August 1973

An F-14A Tomcat from VF-1 lands aboard the *Enterprise*. Note the "100" on the nose and "00" atop the tail; the air wing's "NK" code is carried on the inside surfaces of the twin tail fins. The VF-1 designation is carried on the small, ventral fins, under the fuselage "Navy." When the F-14A went to sea it was the most capable fighter in any service. (U.S. Navy, Don W. Redden)

And, as far as the stated main objective of the entire American involvement in Vietnam—that of saving South Vietnam from a Communist take-over—the fast-moving events of 1975 threw the whole effort right out the window. The United States could only recall its ships, aircraft, and men—and wait.

The final Communist push was not long in coming. Like a cat waiting by the mousehole, the North Vietnamese watched and waited, too, until American support was at such a low state, that any danger from United States' aircraft—which had always been the only real fear of the insurgents—was virtually nonexistent. Cambodia fell first, with elements of the Communist Khmer Rouge and thousands of North Vietnamese and Viet Cong putting an effective stranglehold on Phnom Penh, closing the Mekong to all river traffic. Rocket and artillery fire reached for the airfields and population centers. The feeble efforts of the South Vietnamese Air Force, operating for the first time without its big American patron, were not enough to stem the tide. It was clear that a Communist takeover was within days. Thus, Operation Eagle Pull was initiated and the evacuation of the American embassy was carried out on April 12, 1975 with Marine helicopters of HMH-462 and 463 providing the transport.

The *Midway* and *Enterprise* had been recalled to the South China Sea to cover the operations. The *Enterprise* was on its first deployment with a new fighter aircraft, the F-14A. The recently commissioned VF-1 and 2 had several problems as the first squadrons (outside of the training squadron VF-124) to operate the two-seat Tomcat, but to these two units fell the distinction of operating the brand-new fighter in a combat environment for the first time. As the Communists swept southwards towards Saigon, the F-14s provided fighter cover during Operation Frequent Wind, the final evacuation of Saigon.

The older carriers *Midway, Coral Sea*, and *Hancock*, provided additional support; in the case of *Midway* ten Air Force H-53s were on board to be used as shuttle aircraft. By April 25 the Communists had swept up Hue, Da Nang, Nha Trang, and other South Vietnamese cities, and were virtually on Saigon's doorstep. As A-7s, A-6s, and F-14s from the carriers offshore swept over the city in company

An F-14A Tomcat from VF-1 aboard the *Enterprise* streaks across the sky with wings extended. They sweep back for high-speed flight. The six AIM-54A Phoenix long-range air-to-air missiles nest under the fuselage, between the engine nacelles. The *Enterprise* brought two F-14A squadrons to Vietnamese waters in the spring of 1975 but they were not used in combat. (Robert L. Lawson)

with Marine AH-1J Hueycobras providing low-level escort, the helicopters from the *Midway* began non-stop flights to the beleaguered capital to pick up American and South Vietnamese civilians trying to escape. In what became known as the "Night of the Helicopters" the Sea Stallion made over 40 sorties, bringing over 2,000 people back to the *Midway*.

South Vietnamese aircraft also tried to cover the evacuation. F-5As and A-37s overflew the operation. However, some of these aircraft were piloted by South Vietnamese defectors who had, perhaps prudently, decided to switch sides. There was one

USS *Hancock* (CVA-19), built in 1943 and active throughout the Vietnam War, under way, as two of its RF-8Gs cross its wake. (U.S. Navy)

report of an F-5 wingman turning on his leader in an apparent effort to shoot him down before the planes disappeared from sight. A-1s and AC-119 gunships patrolled at night, trying to catch the flashes of Communist gunfire, but to little avail. Many South Vietnamese pilots apparently did continue to fight for the falling government, covering evacuation operations right up to the morning of April 30. Others escaped with their aircraft, flying the valuable F-5s and A-37s to Thailand; others flew helicopters out to the U.S. ships offshore, jumping from their aircraft, hoping to be rescued by the Americans. One South Vietnamese Air Force major, together with his wife and five children managed to land his Cessna O-1 Bird Dog on the *Midway* after repeated passes to drop a note, requesting permission to land. The deck was eventually cleared and he landed his little propeller-driven observation plane on *Midway*'s deck.

Eventually, nearly 8,000 people—Americans, South Vietnamese employees of American installations, and American security forces—had been evacuated from Saigon by helicopter to the American fleet waiting offshore. American aircraft flew over Saigon during the night of April 29–30. One Corsair pilot remembered the scene.

The city was dying. I glanced north toward Bien Hoa just eighteen miles away where I had spent a year, and where the VC now, presumably, slept in my old hootch.

On April 30, 1975, North Vietnamese tanks

During the final days of South Vietnam and in the *Mayaguez* crisis, reconnaissance aircraft again had an important role. This RF-8G Photo Crusader from VFP-63 aboard the *Midway* was rebuilt from an RF-8A. Note the relatively small area of the wings that fold for carrier stowage. (Hideki Nagakubo)

The Marine Corps' own O-1E Bird Dogs reached the end of their service lives and the Marines had to quickly borrow additional aircraft from the Army, without having time to repaint the two-seat Cessnas in Marine markings. Taken in 1968, this photograph shows two Marine crewmen on a low level photo reconnaissance flight in an O-1E still bearing Army identification. Note the smoke rocket canisters under the wing. (U.S. Marine Corps)

rolled into the city and through the gates of the Presidential Palace. Saigon, and South Vietnam, had fallen to the Communists.

THE MAYAGUEZ INCIDENT

Shortly after the collapse of South Vietnam, American resolve was put to one final test in Southeast Asia. In a move reminiscent of the North Korean seizure of the *Pueblo* in 1968, Cambodian gunboats seized the American merchant ship SS *Mayaguez* on May 12, 1975. The *Mayaguez* was steaming in international waters, heading for Thailand, when she was boarded and her thirty-nine crewmen captured by the newly installed Communist government of Cambodia. Coming fast on the heels of the humiliating fall of Saigon, this brazen act was too much for the American public. President Ford, who had taken over the government from President Nixon less than a year before, felt he had to move quickly. The disaster of Watergate in which Nixon became the first United States President to resign his office, the takeover of South Vietnam, and the general feeling across the country of frustration made a strong, positive action mandatory.

A quickly assembled force of Marine troops and Air Force helicopters hit Koh Tang island off the Cambodian coast at dawn on May 15. The whereabouts of the *Mayaguez* were not known; in fact there had been unsubstantiated reports that the crewmen had been released in small boats in the

317

A rare photo of a Marine TF-9J of Marine Air Group 11 taking off from Da Nang on a reconnaissance mission in 1966. The Marines used these two-seat Cougars for combat missions over South Vietnam while at the same time they were serving as trainers in the United States. (U.S. Marine Corps)

This Marine A-4 Skyhawk is making the first "official" catapult launch from the Marine airfield at Chu Lai on 10 May 1966. During the 1960s the Marines developed catapults, arresting gear, and metal runways for use in forward areas. But most of the massive American complex of airfields built in South Vietnam and Thailand during the 1960s were constructed of concrete. (U.S. Marine Corps)

An EF-10B Skyknight of VMCJ-1 stands in a monsoon rian. These big twin-engined aircraft performed valuable electronic countermeasusre service until 1969 (U.S. Marine Corps)

A-4 Skyhawks during a recovery aboard the carrier *Forrestal*.
(U.S. Navy)

Gulf of Siam, to await rescue. The Sea Stallions unloaded their troops on Koh Tang, to be met with intense mortar and small-arms fire from the Cambodian defenders. Two helos were shot down as they attempted either to take off, or land to unload troops. The three remaining CH-53s of the initial force managed to get back.

More helicopters dropped Marines of the U.S. frigate *Holt* to form a boarding party to storm the *Mayaguez* once it was found. The need was obviated, however, when word was received that the freighter's crew had been released. That left the hard-pressed Marines on Koh Tang, and throughout the day, Navy and Air Force planes struck Ream airfield near Kampong Sam to hold down any Cambodian attempt at reinforcing its contingent on the island. The Marines on the ground were airlifted out by nightfall. Total U.S. casualties were fifteen men killed, three missing and fifty wounded.

The strong U.S. reaction to the seizure of the *Mayaguez*, which was not actually a government-authorized action, apparently secured the crewmen's release. The storming of Koh Tang, the use of American airpower once more, and the eventual return of the merchant sailors dispelled a little of the frustration which most Americans had felt since the fall of South Vietnam. The captain of the *Mayaguez* visited the *Coral Sea* soon after his release to thank the men on the ship for coming to his crew's aid. He said, "If it hadn't been for *Coral Sea* and the destroyers *Wilson* and *Holt*, we probably would be in a Cambodian prison camp today."

With the conclusion of the *Mayaguez* incident,

American presence in Southeast Asia dwindled. Involvement had ended as it had begun nearly eleven years before. An American ship had been attacked on the high seas and elements of the Navy's carrier force had been pressed into service. The United States still maintains carrier patrols in the Western Pacific, but, for all intents and purposes, after a standing presence of thirty years, U.S. carrier aviation in the South China Sea had come to an end.

INDEX

113
VF-213, 103, 105
VFP; see Reconnaissance
squadrons
VMFA-115, 104, 149, 283
VMFA-212, 283
VMFA-232, 283
VMFA-312, 26
VMFA-333, 280
Flaming Dart operations,
42–43, 49
Flynn, Comdr. Sam, 276,
286
Forrestal (CVA-59), 169, 224,
296; fire, 179–183
Franklin D. Roosevelt (CVA-
42), 123, 155
Frishman, Lt. Robert, 240

Garrett County (LST-786),
143
Glenn, Maj. John H., 238
Guadalcanal (LPH-7), 194
Guideline missile; see SA-2
Hancock (CVA-19), 19, 38,
41–43, 45–47, 52, 53,
112, 115, 123, 192, 213,
215–216, 230, 239, 243,
244, 257–261, 265,
268–269, 275, 284,
286–287, 311
Hawkeye (E-2) in Vietnam,
86, 255
Hays, Comdr. Ronald J.,
106
Heinemann, Ed, 209
Helicopter squadrons:
HAL-3, 138–139, 141, 142
HC-7, 178

HM-12, 305
HMH-462, 311
HMH-463, 188, 195, 305,
311
HMM-164, 189, 305
HMM-165, 135, 305
HMM-261, 78
HMM-361, 78
HMM-364, 234
HS-84, 173
Henderson (DD-785), 173
Holloway, Capt. James L.,
III, 91
Holt (DE-1074), 322
Hornet CVS-12), 262

Independence (CVA-62), 64,
67, 81, 84, 90
IOIC (Integrated Operational
Intelligence Center),
220–229; see also Recon-
naissance operations and
Vigilante (RA-5C)
Intrepid (CVS-11), 92, 93,
131, 157, 164, 183, 215
Intruder (A-6) in Vietnam:
A-6A, 82, 84; A-6C, 245;
KA-6D, 245; see also
Prowler (EA-6B)
Iron Hand missions, 64,
208–209, 237–238, 260;
see also Electronic war-
fare operations
Isaacks, Comdr., "Red," 156,
158

John, Lt. William, 286
Johnson, Lt. Clinton, 73
Johnson, Lyndon B., 29, 42,
120, 150, 208–209, 237

329

THE BEST IN SUSPENSE FROM ZEBRA
by Jon Land

THE DOOMSDAY SPIRAL   (1481, $3.50)

Tracing the deadly twists and turns of a plot born in Auschwitz, Alabaster — master assassin and sometime Mossad agent — races against time and operatives from every major service in order to control and kill a genetic nightmare let loose in America!

THE LUCIFER DIRECTIVE   (1353, $3.50)

From a dramatic attack on Hollywood's Oscar Ceremony to the hijacking of three fighter bombers armed with nuclear weapons, terrorists are out-gunning agents and events are outracing governments. Minutes are ticking away to a searing blaze of earth-shattering destruction!

VORTEX   (1469-4, $3.50)

The President of the US and the Soviet Premier are both helpless. Nuclear missiles are hurtling their way to a first strike and no one can stop the top-secret fiasco — except three men with old scores to settle. But if one of them dies, all humanity will perish in a vortex of annihilation!

MUNICH 10   (1300, $3.95)
by Lewis Orde

They've killed her lover, and they've kidnapped her son. Now the world-famous actress is swept into a maelstrom of international intrigue and bone-chilling suspense — and the only man who can help her pursue her enemies is a complete stranger . . .

DEADFALL   (1400, $3.95)
By Lewis Orde and Bill Michaels

The two men Linda cares about most, her father and her lover, entangle her in a plot to hold Manhattan Island hostage for a billion dollars ransom. When the bridges and tunnels to Manhattan are blown, Linda is suddenly a terrorist — except *she's* the one who's terrified!

Available wherever paperbacks are sold, or order direct from the Publisher. Send cover price plus 50¢ per copy for mailing and handling to Zebra Books, Dept. 1749, 475 Park Avenue South, New York, N.Y. 10016. DO NOT SEND CASH.

THE SURVIVALIST SERIES
by Jerry Ahern

ASHES
by William W. Johnstone

OUT OF THE ASHES   (1137, $3.50)
Ben Raines hadn't looked forward to the War, but he knew it was coming. After the balloons went up, Ben was one of the survivors, fighting his way across the country, searching for his family, and leading a band of new pioneers attempting to bring America OUT OF THE ASHES.

FIRE IN THE ASHES   (1310, $3.50)
It's 1999 and the world as we know it no longer exists. Ben Raines, leader of the Resistance, must regroup his rebels and prep them for bloody guerilla war. But are they ready to face an even fiercer foe—the human mutants threatening to overpower the world!

ANARCHY IN THE ASHES   (1387, $3.50)
Out of the smoldering nuclear wreckage of World War III, Ben Raines has emerged as the strong leader the Resistance needs. When Sam Hartline, the mercenary, joins forces with an invading army of Russians, Ben and his people raise a bloody banner of defiance to defend earth's last bastion of freedom.

BLOOD IN THE ASHES   (1537, $3.50)
As Raines and his ragged band of followers search for land that has escaped radiation, the insidious group known as The Ninth Order rises up to destroy them. In a savage battle to the death, it is the fate of America itself that hangs in the balance!

Available wherever paperbacks are sold, or order direct from the Publisher. Send cover price plus 50¢ per copy for mailing and handling to Zebra Books, Dept. 1749, 475 Park Avenue South, New York, N.Y. 10016. DO NOT SEND CASH.

THE SAIGON COMMANDOS SERIES
by Jonathan Cain

#2: CODE ZERO: SHOTS FIRED   (1329, $2.50)

When a phantom chopper pounces on Sergeant Mark Stryker and his men of the 716th, bloody havoc follows. And the sight of the carnage nearly breaks Stryker's control. He will make the enemy pay; they will face his SAIGON COMMANDOS!

#4: CHERRY-BOY BODY BAG   (1407, $2.50)

Blood flows in the streets of Saigon when Sergeant Mark Stryker's MPs become targets for a deadly sniper. Surrounded by rookies, Stryker must somehow stop a Cong sympathizer from blowing up a commercial airliner—without being blown away by the crazed sniper!

#5: BOONIE-RAT BODY BURNING   (1441, $2.50)

Someone's torching GIs in a hellhole known as Fire Alley and Sergeant Stryker and his MPs are in on the manhunt. To top it all off, Stryker's got to keep the lid on the hustlers, deserters, and Cong sympathizers who make his beat the toughest in the world!

#6: DI DI MAU OR DIE   (1493, $2.50)

The slaughter of a U.S. payroll convoy means it's up to Sergeant Stryker and his men to take on the Vietnamese mercenaries the only way they know how: with no mercy and with M-16s on full automatic!

#7: SAC MAU, VICTOR CHARLIE   (1574, $2.50)

Stryker's war cops, ordered to provide security for a movie being shot on location in Saigon, are suddenly out in the open and easy targets. From that moment on it's Lights! Camera! Bloodshed!

Available wherever paperbacks are sold, or order direct from the Publisher. Send cover price plus 50¢ per copy for mailing and handling to Zebra Books, Dept. 1749, 475 Park Avenue South, New York, N.Y. 10016. DO NOT SEND CASH.